SCRAPBOOKING FAMILY MEMORIES

All New Page Ideas Celebrating
Special Occasions and Everyday Moments

MEMORY MAKERS BOOKS

Managing Editor maryjo regier
Senior Editor lydia rueger
Art Director nick nyffeler
Graphic Designers jordan kinney, robin rozum
Associate Editor amy glander
Art Acquisitions Editor janetta abucejo wieneke
Craft Editor jodi amidei
Photographer ken trujillo
Contributing Photographers jennifer reeves
Photo Stylist kevin hardiek
Contributing Writer elizabeth shaffer harlan
Editorial Support karen cain, emily curry hitchingham, dena twinem
Contributing Memory Makers Masters jessie baldwin, joanna bolick, jenn brookover, christine brown, susan cyrus, lisa dixon, sheila doherty, kathy fesmire, diana graham, angie head, jeniece higgins, nicola howard, julie johnson, kelli noto, torrey scott, trudy sigurdson, shannon taylor, denise tucker, andrea lyn vetten-marley, samantha walker, sharon whitehead

Memory Makers® Scrapbooking Family Memories

Published by Memory Makers Books, an imprint of F+W Publications, Inc.
12365 Huron Street, Suite 500, Denver, CO 80234
Phone (800) 254-9124
First edition. Printed in the United States.
09 08 07 06 05 5 4 3 2 1

Library of Congress Cataloging-in-Publication Data

Scrapbooking family memories : all new page ideas celebrating special occasions and
everyday moments.
p. cm.
Includes index.
ISBN 1-892127-59-8
1. Photographs--Conservation and restoration. 2. Photograph albums. 3. Scrapbooks. 4.
Photography of families. I. Memory Makers Books.

TR465.S3943 2005
745.593--dc22

2005049562

Distributed to trade and art markets by
F+W Publications, Inc.
4700 East Galbraith Road, Cincinnati, OH 45236
Phone (800) 289-0963
ISBN 1-892127-59-8

Distributed in Canada by Fraser Direct
100 Armstrong Avenue
Georgetown, ON, Canada L7G 5S4
Tel: (905) 877-4411

Distributed in the U.K. and Europe by David & Charles
Brunel House, Newton Abbot, Devon, TQ12 4PU, England
Tel: (+44) 1626 323200, Fax: (+44) 1626 323319
E-mail: mail@davidandcharles.co.uk

Distributed in Australia by Capricorn Link
P.O. Box 704, S. Windsor NSW, 2756 Australia
Tel: (02) 4577-3555

Memory Makers Books is the home of *Memory Makers*, the scrapbook magazine dedicated to educating and inspiring scrapbookers.
To subscribe, or for more information, call (800) 366-6465. Visit us on the Internet at www.memorymakersmagazine.com.

This book belongs to

_____

This book is dedicated to our Memory Makers contributors who celebrate the ones they love most in scrapbooks.

table of contents

mothers

fathers

immediate family

introduction

Last Christmas when I was expecting our first child, a home décor plaque in a catalog caught my eye. In a flowing yet comfortable script it read, "Home is where your story begins." I looked around our home and thought back on all the painting, remodeling and decorating we'd done in the past three years to make this 35-year-old house look like "us," from the red-orange color of the living room walls that I love to our vintage ski poster that took forever to find. And I was proud that our child's story will begin in this place. She will take her first steps here; celebrate her first Christmas here; cry, laugh and love here; learn to smile for the camera here. It's exciting for me to think that the start of her life story also marks the beginning of our family.

From the infancy of creative scrapbooking to the present day, family is often what spurs people to begin preserving their memories. Many started because they wanted to document their wedding or the birth of their first child in a special way. But even if you're not a wife or a mother, you're a daughter, a sister, a cousin, an aunt or a pet owner. You've hosted or attended family events, and you remember the feelings associated with your first family home. Whoever you are, you are part of a family that deserves to be celebrated and will identify with the project ideas in *Scrapbooking Family Memories*.

In this jampacked book, we've included chapters on mothers, fathers, immediate family, extended family, family gatherings, family homes and family pets. Each chapter begins with a short personal anecdote from a featured artist that will help spark memories of interesting situations and humorous events among your own relatives. At the end of each chapter, you'll find fun mini-album ideas to re-create as gifts for any family member. In addition, you'll discover new and innovative family-related scrapbook products and ways to use them on pages 8-9 as well as tips for scrapbooking family memories on pages 10-11.

We hope the ideas in *Scrapbooking Family Memories* will help you discover new ways to record your ever-unfolding family tale. As the "stories" of your family life grow and change through the years, may the plot thicken along with your albums!

Lydia

Lydia Rueger, Senior Editor

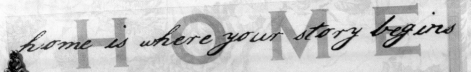

HOME

home is where your story begins

My family story with Derek began at 4821 West 29th Avenue in Northwest Denver—the first place we lived after we were married. It was us and the cat at the time, and I was so excited to live in an old Victorian house, even if we were just renting. I liked to imagine all the other family stories that had started there, too, in the nearly 110 years since the home was built.

June 2001

What we loved:

The secret, tiny room with the built-in bookshelves upstairs

The white picket fence • The hardwood floors

The French doors to the livingroom, complete with antique key hole

The stained-glass windows • Running at Sloans Lake

Walking to our favorite Mexican restaurant, La Concinita

Going to open houses in the neighborhood

Being close to the shops and restaurants at 32nd and Lowell

supplies for making lasting albums

The use of high-quality scrapbook materials will ensure your cherished family memories stay the course of time.

we recommend the following:

- *Archival-quality albums*

- *PVC-free page protectors*

- *Acid- and lignin-free papers*

- *Acid-free and photo-safe adhesives*

- *Pigment-ink pens and markers*

- *PVC-free memorabilia keepers, sleeves or envelopes*

- *Flat, photo-safe embellishments (encapsulate or place away from photos if questionable)*

- *De-acidifying spray for news clippings or documents*

how to create a scrapbook page from the background out

Start with a selection of photos for a single page and gather any appropriate memorabilia. Select a background paper that pulls one color from your photos or establishes the mood you wish to convey. You may wish to choose additional papers that complement your theme or photos. Pick out or make page additions that complement photos if desired. Loosely assemble photos, title, journaling, memorabilia and page accents to form a visually appealing layout. Trim and mat photos, then mount in place with adhesive. Add title and journaling. Complete the page with any additional accents. For instructions on how to replicate the above page exactly, see page 124.

albums

Scrapbook albums come in a variety of styles. These can include post-bound, strap-hinge, three-ring binder and spiral as well as a variety of sizes from 4 x 6" to 12 x 15". Find one that best suits your shelf space and works well with your personal scrapbooking style.

paper

Paper is available in solid cardstock as well as a variety of patterns and also as speciality papers including vellum, suede, mulberry, handmade paper and metallics. For versatile back-grounds, accents and photo mats, incorporate coordinating patterns and themed papers to lend additional artistic flair perfect for family pages. Use only acid- and lignin-free papers to protect your photos and memorabilia and to ensure your albums have an extra-long shelf life.

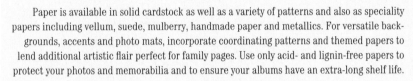

embellishments

Tags, beads, ribbons, fibers, charms, stickers, metal accents and other adorn-ments are used to decorate and add flair to scrapbook pages. Combine them or use them alone for customized decorating.

adhesives

Scrapbook adhesives are manufactured to ensure strong binding of photos, memorabilia and embellishments to scrapbook papers without damaging photographs. They are available in a variety of forms including glue pens and sticks, photo splits, spray adhesives and tape runners. Some varieties on the market offer permanent bonding; others allow you to remove photos at a later date if you should have the need.

pens and markers

From fine-point to large brush styles, these are used for journaling as well as for adding decorative flourishes to page design. Choose writing tools that are safe for scrapbooking. Practice using your writing tool on scrap paper before writing directly on your scrapbook page.

tips for scrapbooking family memories

photo duplication

You may wish to make duplicates of your photos for family members. This could include heritage photos or photos taken using a 35mm camera before the digital boom. Fortunately, today's technology offers several quick and easy do-it-yourself options that make photo duplication easy.

Photo duplication machines offer one of the simplest and most economic methods. In a matter of minutes, these machines create photo-quality reprints in a variety of sizes without requiring a negative. Photo duplication machines also allow you to crop your photos, correct red-eye and adjust the brightness and color contrast.

It's also possible to create photo duplicates by taking pictures of the originals. This provides negatives that can be copied as often as you like. For best results, you'll need special equipment: an SLR camera, a macro lens and a copy stand. However, good copies of 5 x 7" and 8 x 10" photos can also be created by using a manual-focus 35mm or 50mm camera and sufficient sunlight. Your local camera store can provide you with more detailed information and may also rent equipment.

If you're up-to-date with digital technology, you can make your own duplicates simply by using a computer, a scanner and a compatible photo software program. Prints can be made from scanned photos and the images stored on disk or CD until further reprints are desired.

quotes, phrases & sayings

In the whirlwind of family life, it can often be a challenge to find the right words to grace your scrapbook pages. Using a favorite quote or lyric on a scrapbook page can express an emotion or feeling that you cannot express in your own words.

There are many sources for finding quotes and other sentiments. One option is to purchase small quote booklets or stickers that relate to your theme. These can be found at hobby chain stores or in your local scrapbooking store. Another option is to search for your subject on quote-related Web sites, in poetry books, in the Bible and even on T-shirts, buttons and bumper stickers. Carrying a notebook and pen with you in your purse or backpack is another good way to record punchy words, jokes or phrases you may overhear en route to work or in line at the supermarket.

These Web sites offer thousands of quotes, many sorted by theme:

www.famous-quotations.com
www.quotegarden.com
www.quotationspage.com
www.quoteland.com
www.brainyquote.com
www.goodquotes.com
www.wisdomquotes.com
www.lost45s.com (early rock song lyrics)

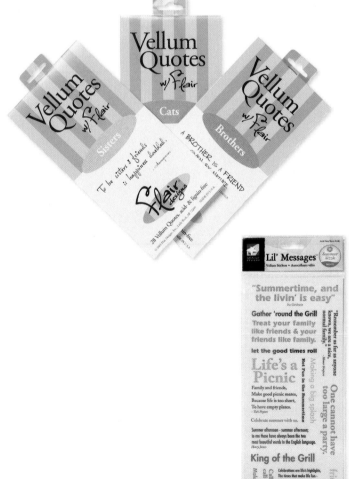

journaling

Most scrapbookers have a wealth of family stories to tell. Fitting all the information on the page may present a spacial challenge. Rest assured there are many simple and fun ways to journal your family's story. Your journaling represents your personal connection to the photos on the page and also shares the story and circumstances behind the photo. In generations to come, your descendants will thank you for taking the time to elaborate on the story elements.

If you are searching for some ways to get your creative journaling energy from mind to paper, try utilizing some of these sources. Chances are good you already have them in your possession. One good source is letters or e-mails from family members, including the traditional holiday letters sharing a year's worth of events. Video and sound recordings from weddings, birthday parties, holiday gatherings and other occasions is probably the most realistic and accurate account of experiences you could get your hands on. Bulletins from special occasions such as weddings, graduations, school plays and holiday pageants, cards with special messages addressed to loved ones, journals or diaries, postcards, birth announcements, wedding announcements and newspaper clippings all share valuable information that can be used in sharing your story on your scrapbook page.

Bullet journaling and paragraph journaling are two types most commonly seen in family scrapbooks. With bullet or list journaling, you can include a lot of information in a smaller amount of space. Use the title to state the main point or question that is answered in the bullets to avoid repetition. The scrapbook page shown at left is a good example. Standard paragraph journaling is great if you have a lot of information you would like to include. Remember to leave a line of space between each paragraph so the text is easy to read and does not clutter your page design.

more fun ideas

Use your scrapbook supplies to create fun family projects such as photo name tags or place cards for family reunions or other occasions. You can also use your supplies to craft invitations to gatherings large or small. Or make a mini album, copy it multiple times and give it to everyone in your family. If the scrapping bug runs in the family, you can start a circle journal with your family as the theme. Pages in the front can be heritage pages with black-and-white photos of grandparents or ancestors. As the journal gets passed, each family can create pages that showcase the moments and milestones in their lives.

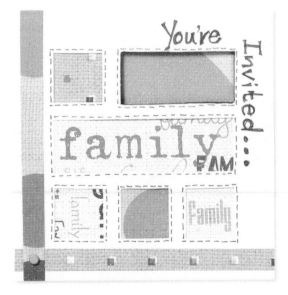

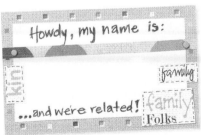

mothers

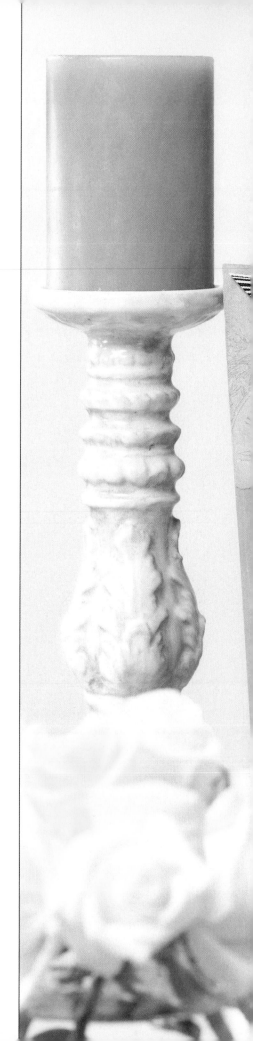

CHAPTER ONE

A mother looks at her children with a perfect love. She supports our dreams, calms our fears, mends our wounded hearts and encourages us to be unique individuals in a world where conformity is ubiquitous. She can make a mean grilled cheese, offer marital advice, knows many inventive ways to calm a crying baby and teaches us how to balance a fulfilling career with a growing family. She is our cheerleader through life from the first day of kindergarten to the day we bring our own offspring into the world. Whether she's serving up a plate of motherly wisdom or her famous meatloaf, her grace, honesty and integrity serve as a guiding hand through all of life's struggles, discoveries and joys.

There's no better way to celebrate motherhood than through a scrapbook page dedicated to the delight and adventure that come with it. Whether you are a soccer mom, career mom, Pilates mom or jack-of-all-trades mom, you deserve a page all about you. Dedicate a page to your own mother or to the enchantment your children bring to your life.

We were so proud the day my mother-in-law accomplished her lifelong goal of graduating from college. When we asked her what made her most excited about the experience, she said that she was glad to be able to finally spend more time with family, especially her grandchildren.

—Jeniece Higgins

"Motherhood: All love begins and ends there."

—*Robert Browning*

when i became a mother

Leah says, "Motherhood has been one of the most amazing experiences of my life, so I knew I had to create a special layout for this subject." She told her story through expansive journaling, remarking about bonding with her son before he was born and about how her long labor and C-section brought a beautiful, healthy boy. To add a sweet memory to the page, Leah included a hand- and footprint of her newborn.

Leah LaMontagne, Las Vegas, Nevada

Supplies: Patterned papers, scrapbook molding, tags, square metal fasteners (Chatterbox); letter stamps (Hero Arts); silver conchos (Scrapworks); flower charm (American Traditional Designs); blue satin ribbon (Offray); white cardstock; blue pigment ink; clear embossing powder; blue pen

Me & Shell
Shell & Meg

just like me

Family and friends often rave about similarities between moms and kids, but mommies don't always see it. Lily snuggled up next to her daughter and took this photo. "When I really looked at the picture," she says, "the similarities just jumped out at me. That got me thinking about all the little ways our personalities are similar." Lily wrote the list of shared traits but then put it aside. A few days later, she received a monthly scrapbooking kit in the mail that contained the papers she used to finish the page.

Lily Goldsmith, Orlando, Florida

Supplies: Patterned papers, journaling block (KI Memories); wooden frame, flowers and letters (Li'l Davis Designs); letter stamps (FontWerks, Ma Vinci's Reliquary); dye ink (Ranger); dark and light pink cardstocks (Bazzill); green eyelets

a daughter is . . .

Krista's page emphasizes the great friendship she shares with her mother. Her mom invited her to a day at the beach and, "At first I didn't want to go on the trip because I had lots of work to do," she says, "but my mom convinced me that a day at the beach with family was just the thing I needed to relax and have some fun." The trip accomplished just that. She highlighted her photo by folding ribbon over two corners. To keep elements cohesive, she painted metal embellishments, brads and a charm with pink paint.

Krista Fernandez, Fremont, California
Photo: April Bibbins, Livermore, California

Supplies: Patterned papers (KI Memories); ribbons (Li'l Davis Designs, Offray, SEI); flower brads, metal flower charm, jewelry tags (Making Memories); rub-on letters (Scrapworks); turquoise and white cardstocks; staples; pink acrylic paint; black pen

I have fallen in love with my daughter

I thank God for her endearing qualities. I love how she tries on my glasses, says "kanfus" in thanks, shares with her brother, asks for "big hugs", and wants to spend time with me.

the soul is healed by being with children

DOSTOEVSKY

in love with my daughter

Mothering has ups and downs. When Rosemary is having a tough day, she says, "It really helps to focus on the things I love about my kids. I make note of the little things that bring me bits of joy." To create this page, she journaled some of those sweet thoughts above a photo that captured a sweet moment between mother and daughter. She added stickers for a title and a bit of color.

Rosemary Waits, Mustang, Oklahoma

Supplies: Patterned paper (Karen Foster Design); star, quote and letter stickers (Creative Imaginations); distress ink (Ranger); gray and white cardstocks (Bazzill); black pen

I am Colleen Marie Margaret Culleiton Stearns. I was born the first daughter of Thomas and Susan Culleiton on March 21, 1969. I became wife of James Curtis Stearns on February 15, 1992. On June 20, 1997, I became the mother of Jacob Charles Stearns, and my second child Ian James Stearns was born on June 6, 2000. As of today, October 31, 2004, I have many friends, all of whom I met online. In all of my roles, I am blessed.

what my roles are

For one of the pages in Colleen's "About Me" album, she wanted future generations to know the various roles she performed at 35 years old. Her journaling tells the story from the first person in the form of a news story about the important people and events that shaped those roles. For a rich design, she surrounded black-and-white photos with warm browns and rich velvet ribbon.

Colleen Stearns, Natrona Heights, Pennsylvania

Supplies: Patterned paper (Autumn Leaves); brown velvet ribbon (Scrapping With Style); rub-on letters, letter tiles (Making Memories); label maker (Dymo); rust and tan cardstocks (Bazzill); black hinges; black mini brads; brown stamping ink

WIFE MOTHER SISTER DAUGHTER FRIEND WIFE MOTHER

what my ROLES are

being a step-mom

Kathy often designs pages about her stepdaughter, Alex, but she wanted to create one that expressed how much she loves her. Keeping the title phrase in mind, Kathy journaled about her. She then e-mailed the text to Alex at college with a description of the page. She asked her to write about how she feels about their relationship. "When I got her response," Kathy says, "I could barely read it through my tears. I knew she loved me, but it was very moving to read about all the things she remembered about my parenting." Silk flowers and pastel colors add a feminine touch to Kathy's page.

Kathy Fesmire, Athens, Tennessee

Supplies: Patterned papers (Leaving Prints); chipboard letters (Westrim); foam letter stamps, label holder, rub-on letters (Making Memories); chenille fringe and ribbons (Offray); pink cardstock; pink, silver and yellow paints; silk flowers; transparency

the momma

Santa brought Alison's daughter a camera for Christmas and this trio of earthquake photos were some of the first shots from it. Alison loved how they captured a two year old's perspective. She says, "I tried to keep my journaling from the same perspective." When designing, Alison tends to look for colors and patterns before themes. For this page, she wanted a mostly black paper with a large design. She spotted this pop top paper and put it to great use.

Alison Chabe, Charlestown, Massachusetts
Photos: James Chabe, Charlestown, Massachusetts

Supplies: Patterned papers (Out There Scrapbooking, Scrapworks); corner rounder (Creative Memories); rub-on letters (ChartPak, Creative Imaginations); watermark yellow ink (Tsukineko); red and white cardstocks

mommy and talon

Sometimes knowing that a baby is the last one to be born in a family makes parents hold on to every moment. Scrapbookers create pages as an outlet to these feelings and as a way to capture and save those precious moments. As Michelle's last baby grows, she says "I thought these moments were bittersweet . . . I love and cherish every moment." Michelle's digital page contains papers she designed in image-editing software. She says "I created the design before I took the picture, but once I saw it, I knew it was perfect."

Michelle Underwood, Paris, Tennessee
Photo: Danny Underwood, Paris, Tennessee

Supplies: Image-editing software (Jasc Paint Shop Pro)

so happy you found me

Jackie's son, almost 5 now, has Asperger's Syndrome, a form of autism with normal functioning speech and development, but social challenges, making it difficult to understand feelings. In the journaling, she says, "People with Asperger's have a hard time with eye contact. It makes them uncomfortable and causes them to lose their train of thought. So, the day my son looked me in the eye and said, 'I Love You' was a huge moment in my life." Jackie created a graphic look by handcutting the title, rounding corners and adding two punched and pieced hearts.

Jackie Siperko, Dallas, Pennsylvania

Supplies: Heart punch (EK Success); circle and wave cutting system (Creative Memories); white, cocoa, avocado, turquoise and dark brown cardstocks; hole punch

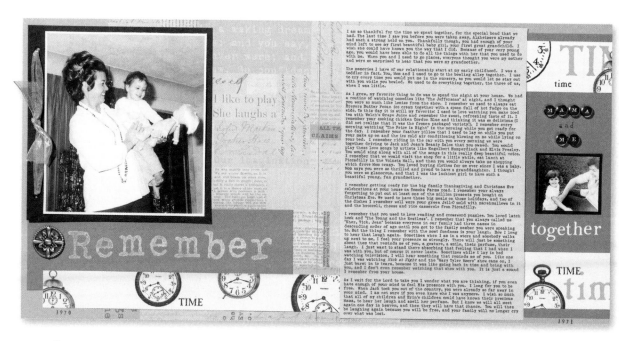

remember

Jeannie's journaling chronicles a lifetime of strong memories and shared moments with her grandmother. She wrote in a large journaling block about everyday activities such as watching television shows together, riding with her to work and listening to music on the radio. She captured little things that still trigger fresh memories. To balance the weight of the journaling block, she used a strong focal-point photo and title.

Jeannie van Wert, Tampa, Florida
Photos: Sherry Bradley, Ormond Beach, Florida

Supplies: Patterned papers (KI Memories, Rusty Pickle); metal embellishment (EK Success); letter stamps (Hero Arts, Ma Vinci's Reliquary); conchos (Scrapworks); date stamp (Making Memories); white, black, gray, blue and powder blue cardstocks (Bazzill); white and black dye inks; white letter stickers; silver ribbon

a sign of love

Linda captured a midsummer moment outside with her niece. While snapping the shutter, she asked the children to give their mom a big kiss, and to her delight, she captured this moment. She put the photo together with a quote. "Whenever I come across a quote that I like, I write it in my notebook. I thought this quote by Shakespeare was perfect, especially since getting my nephew to kiss his mom was so unexpected!" Her page emulated the summer day with fresh colors and floral accents.

Linda Garrity, Kingston, Massachusetts

Supplies: Patterned paper, stencil letter (Autumn Leaves); polka-dot ribbons (May Arts); letter stickers (K & Company, Me & My Big Ideas, Mrs. Grossman's); letter stamps (Hero Arts); date stamp (Making Memories); sky blue and yellow cardstocks (Bazzill); white paint; silk flowers; white brads; transparency; black stamping ink

moments

Sandie often scrapbooks with a friend who owns a scrapbooking store. One day, they decided on a quick getaway to the beach to see another scrapbooking friend. "We piled three kids and two adults into my little Pontiac Vibe and hit the road," she says. To showcase the photo of her other friend, Cindy, with her daughter, Sandie designed a page using bold patterned papers with feminine touches such as ribbons.

Sandie Blair, Glendale, Arizona
Photos: Kim Mattina, Phoenix, Arizona

Supplies: Patterned papers (7 Gypsies, Carolee's Creations, KI Memories); ribbon (May Arts); printed transparency (Creative Imaginations); rub-on letters (Creative Imaginations, Making Memories); black envelope (Li'l Davis Designs); paper flower, decorative brad (Making Memories); letter stickers (Sticker Studio); domino sticker (EK Success); woven label (Chatterbox); black stamping ink; sandpaper; staples

becoming a mother

Shaunte created this spread for an "All About Me" album. "I wanted my children and future generations to know my thoughts and feelings on becoming a mother," she says. Her journaling chronicles her dreaming of being a mom, her transition to becoming one as her first child was born plus many of the joys and challenges of everyday life with five children. To allow the journaling to stand out, Shaunte printed it onto a transparency and embossed it with clear embossing powder. Using acrylic paint, she highlighted a sentence at the end of each paragraph.

Shaunte Wadley, Lehi, Utah
Photos: Sam Wadley, Lehi, Utah

Supplies: Patterned papers (Daisy D's, Making Memories, Outdoors & More Scrapbook Décor); foam letter stamps, metal label holder (Making Memories); date stamp (Office Max); photo turns (7 Gypsies); brown gingham ribbon (Midori); jump rings; charms; cream acrylic paint; clear and gold embossing powder; gold pigment ink; gold brads and eyelets; transparency

maternity clothes

The first few months of pregnancy bring many emotional changes and feelings, usually for the whole family, not just for the mommy. Maria created pages to record various family thoughts and sentiments about that time of transition. She printed her impressions onto cardstock and embellished each tag with black stamping ink. She says, "Since I knew it would be my last time being pregnant, I wanted to document my maternity clothes. The hidden tag talks about my love/hate relationship with them."

Maria Burke, Steinbach, Manitoba, Canada
Photo: Phil Burke, Steinbach, Manitoba, Canada

Supplies: Patterned papers (Chatterbox, Daisy D's, KI Memories, Scrapbook Wizard); photo turns, printed twill (7 Gypsies); gingham ribbon (Offray); journaling tag (www.twopeasinabucket.com); date stamp (Office Depot); ribbons (May Arts); square brad (Creative Impressions); jute twine; brown and tan cardstocks; staples; black stamping ink

snapshots of life

Everyday moments with Mommy are sometimes the sweetest of all. Summer's page shares one such moment her husband captured on film. She built the page around a photo box divider, "because these are the moments that my life consists of most, a true snapshot of my life," she says. For a timeless look, she printed the photo onto textured cardstock and framed it with a variety of label stickers.

Summer Ford, Bulverde, Texas

Supplies: Pink patterned paper, label words, letter stickers, antique pewter chain (Pebbles); letter stamps (Hero Arts); black and cream cardstocks; photo box divider card; brads; fibers; black stamping ink

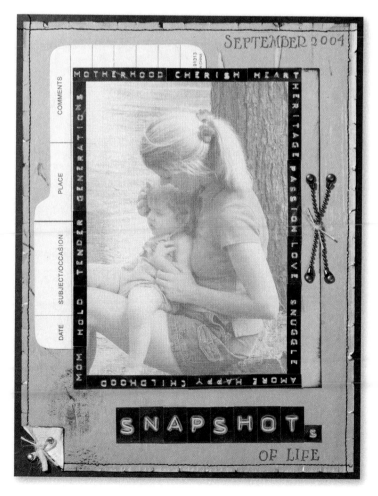

mother daughter

A friend took this special photo of Diana and Karee, her daughter, while on a trip to New York City. It gives a glimpse of the similar features that the two share. Diana says, "We share so much together not only as mother–daughter but as friends." She designed the page, emphasizing their favorite color—pink. The photo's sepia tones coordinate with the layout but draw the eye toward itself as the focal point of the page.

Diana Furey, Malvern, Ohio

Supplies: Patterend papers (Autumn Leaves, Creative Imaginations); decorative brad, metal letters (Making Memories); ribbons (May Arts); wooden letters (Li'l Davis Designs); silk flower

savor the moments

Bubble gum is a fascination and mystery to little ones, and being goofy ranks as a high priority. Shawn took advantage of both these truths while she played with sweet little Paige. "She loved it when I would blow a bubble and let her pop it with her mouth. It was like our little bubble kiss," Shawn says. She designed this digital layout with elements she found on a CD and online, using graphic patterned papers and a fun quote.

Shawn Ostrowski, Zeeland, Michigan

Supplies: Papers and elements (www.playonelements.com); brushwork (www.1greeneye.net); circle brushes (Rhonna Farrer/Dreamy Scrapper)

mother's day 2004

Even when a woman becomes a mother, it does not always meet one's expectations and dreams of what it might entail. Summer never imagined a life full of boys, but this layout, dedicated to one of her favorite photos, tells the story. "I wrote the journaling directly to my boys. I want them to know that I have grown to love being a mom of boys. They teach me new things each and every day," she says. Summer's design features classic images with rich colors and fibers.

Summer Ford, Bulverde, Texas

Supplies: Patterned and vinyl papers, embossed accents, rivets, metal tags (K & Company); distress ink (Ranger); foam letter stamps (Making Memories); fibers, ribbons (Great Balls of Fiber); black and cream cardstocks (Bazzill); label maker (Dymo); tan acrylic paint; black stamping ink

priceless

Kimberly recorded a special Mother's Day full of memories by spoofing a popular advertising campaign. Her focal-point photo tells much of the story of how proud her daughter was to give the gift, but her journaling block tells the "Priceless" punch line. To echo the page theme in her design, she included silk flowers. A pull-out journaling tag recounts the day of celebration.

Kimberly Billings, East Troy, Wisconsin

Supplies: Patterned papers, paper flowers (Making Memories); printed vellum (EK Success); copper mesh (Magic Mesh); evergreen, yellow and white cardstocks; gold brads; yellow eyelet; yellow ribbon; date stamp; black stamping ink

the reason

When Shannon heard the song "The Reason," by Hoobastank, it brought to mind some of the choices she had made in her life. She says, "Having a child made me want to be a better person, someone my son will be proud of when he is older." She created this page using some of the lyrics from the song, and she embellished it with various office supplies, a transparency and a stamped title.

Shannon Bastian, Haubstadt, Indiana
Song lyrics: Hoobastank

Supplies: Patterned paper (Mustard Moon); foam letter stamps (Making Memories); printed transparency (K & Company); definitions (Making Memories); rub-on letters (Li'l Davis Designs); rub-on date (Autumn Leaves); decorative paper clip (EK Success); letter tiles (source unknown); plastic file tab; library pocket and card; black acrylic paint; letter stickers; black brads; red, tan and gray cardstocks

mothers hold their children's hands . . .

On a beach trip, Miki's husband played with their new digital camera. She says, "I thought he was only taking photos of the beautiful sunset, so it was a wonderful surprise to see this photo. He captured such a quiet, peaceful, end-of-the-day moment between Tyler and me. To this day it is one of our favorites." Miki searched for a quote to capture her feelings and eventually found one among her stickers. Since the sticker was the wrong design, she mixed stickers and stamps that she had on hand to create the poem embellishment.

Miki Benedict, Modesto, California
Photo: Keith Benedict, Modesto, California

Supplies: Patterned papers, tags (Basic Grey); die cut (Pebbles); letter stickers (Creative Imaginations, Me & My Big Ideas); letter stamps (Making Memories, Purple Onion Designs); silk ribbon; gold brad; black stamping ink

. . . being your mommy

Journaling about a photo after several years provides opportunities for reflection. Dee says, "I didn't take any notes or write any journaling about those photos. I can't remember the specific details about them . . . but I do have very significant thoughts and feelings now." As she began to design this page, she decided that "my current thoughts and feelings are much more precious, honest and important than trying to just write down the who, what, when and where." She used a zigzag stitch to sew matching patterned papers to her background.

Dee Gallimore-Perry, Griswold, Connecticut
Photos: Robert Perry, Griswold, Connecticut

Supplies: Patterned papers, die cuts, acrylic circles (KI Memories); letter stamps (Turtle Press); love charm (source unknown); grosgrain ribbon; yellow cardstock; paper clip; chalk; black stamping ink; black pen

two of a kind

Children are often the spitting image of their parents. Dee's son is no exception, and the similarities don't stop at their looks. Dee created this page, featuring black and white page elements, to highlight the many ways the two are similar. She enlisted her son to help create the list. To balance the design she used papers that feature line designs in both a negative and positive image. For the title, she stamped onto the black background with white ink.

Dee Gallimore-Perry, Griswold, Connecticut
Photos: Robert Perry, Griswold, Connecticut

Supplies: Patterned papers, die cuts, number stickers, white buckle (KI Memories); clear page pebbles (Making Memories); letter stamps (Turtle Press); label maker (Dymo); black cardstock; black embroidery floss; white stamping ink

1. passing down of *beliefs* and *customs* from one generation to the next 2. *long estab* ...

TRADITION

PIE is happiness

ALL THAT IT CLAIMS TO BE

simple delight

MOMS

There are many ways to eat pie the Allred way.

pre-cious (presh'as) *adj.* of great price or value; costly; highly esteemed.

PIE secrets

Mom learned how to make pies from her mom, Ruth Johnson (Nana). Nana was born in Japan. Her parents were Swedish missionaries. They sent Nana and her sister Hannah, to the United States to be raised by friends. Nana worked as a cook for the family she lived with. She spent countless hours perfecting her pies and Swedish pastries. This wonderful skill she passed down to my mom.

There are many ways to eat pie, let me share with you the Allred way.
1. Best to eat pie when your hungry, so consider pie an appetizer.
2. Turn off the TV, radio and if people around you are talking ask them to observe a moment of silence so that you are not distracted while enjoying your pie.
3. It is true that the first bite is the best. I recommend smelling your piece of pie first so that your anticipation builds before taking that first bite.
4. Take your time while eating your pie, unless of course, you're concerned that the rest of the pie will be eaten if you eat slowly, in this case, scarf down your first piece and slowly savour your second.

mom's pie secrets

Every Thanksgiving, Sande's mom travels to their home to celebrate and to make her famous pies. She says her mother "hits the ground cooking (rather than running). Before her suitcase even makes it to her room, she has an apron on and is making crusts." Sande's sons go to the airport to put in their requests on the way home. Designing this page came quickly as Sande had ideas before starting. She used a file folder to symbolize recipes, lace and collage papers to emphasize tradition and some pie names to demonstrate the range of her mom's talents.

Sande Krieger, Salt Lake City, Utah

RASPBERRY CREAM

LEMON MERINGUE

CARAMEL ALMOND

CHOCOLATE CREAM

BANANA CREAM

PUMPKIN

PECAN

APPLE

PEAR

MINCE

COCONUT CREAM

On the way home from picking her up at the airport, she begins quizzing me. "Do you have shortening? What about lemons? Cream of tartar?" She writes on the envelope her plane ticket was in, listing the ingredients I need to get at the store. She walks into my kitchen setting her purse on the counter and reachs into the drawer for an apron.

The Pie Making has Offically Begun!

An hour later, smells are drifting through the house. Not just any smells, but fabulous, mouth-watering pie smells. We are about to embark on a pie marathon! Glorious day after day of pie eating. Mike and the boys don't stand a chance! I've been training since I was a child. Regularly eating enormous amounts of pie for 40+ years has made me the ultimate pie eating athlete.

Supplies: Patterned papers (Deluxe Designs, K & Company); definitions, rub-on words, foam letter stamps, decorative brads (Making Memories); letter stickers, envelope, die-cut letters (Foofala); copper buckles, star paper clip (Nunn Design); twill tape (7 Gypsies); mini safety pins (Li'l Davis Designs); red grosgrain ribbon (Offray); lace trim; faux buttons; distress ink (Ranger); brown textured paper (source unknown); heart brads (Creative Impressions); metal charm (All My Memories); brown, rust, white and tan cardstocks; brown fibers; red gingham ribbon, white embroidery floss; staples; red acyrlic paint

mom

Jodi created a mini album paying special tribute to her mother, Jane. Each page gives a glimpse into Jane's unique character and the many roles she plays—mother, wife, grandmother and friend. The journaling shares how she has touched everyone around her with her courage, warmth, kindred grace and unconditional love. Jodi printed her journaling on pink cardstock and used a circle-cutting system to trim into large and small circles. Pink and black polka-dot ribbons add a feminine touch.

Jodi Amidei, Memory Makers Books

Supplies: Album (Chatterbox); patterned papers (7 Gypsies, Autumn Leaves, Rusty Pickle); rub-on letters (Rusty Pickle); die-cut letters (QuicKutz); foam letter stamps (Westrim); plastic letters (Colorbök); eyelets (Family Treasures); decorative brads (Making Memories); circle-cutting system (Creative Memories); ribbons (Offray); label maker (Dymo); tea dye varnish (Delta); acrylic paint; staples

fathers

CHAPTER TWO

Dads are special people. Their strength and wisdom guide us, their zest for life inspires us and their kindness and character warms us. Dad is a pal who watches our favorite Saturday morning cartoons with us, a teacher who is always willing to show us one more time how to shoot that free throw and a guiding hand when life presents challenges more difficult than we could have ever imagined.

With all its joy and laughter, it stands to reason that fatherhood deserves a special place in scrapbook albums. Pages can feature tender moments between a little girl and the man who will always be her hero or the exciting times when a little guy accompanies his dad to a baseball game. No one has a bigger heart than Dad so capture his extraordinary character in pages dedicated just to him.

This photo is from the day Dad and I went to Sea World. It has always struck a chord with me because we look so in tune with each other— like we're best buddies.

—Danielle Thompson

"My father gave me the greatest gift anyone could give another person. He believed in me."

—*Jim Valvano*

a father's love

Lisa's family often takes walks near their house, and she enjoys designing pages about these jaunts. She says, "The moment I read this poem it made me think of this day on the nature trail, how Jason interacts with the children and how much they love him for it." She balanced the photos with the heartfelt poem by using muted, neutral tones.

Lisa Sanders, Grain Valley, Missouri

Supplies: Patterned paper (Pebbles, Rusty Pickle); definition stickers, twill patterned stickers (Pebbles); concho letters (Colorbök); photo turns (Making Memories); twill letters (Carolee's Creations); white, black and tan cardstocks; silver brads; chalk

daddy's girl

Marla, who is creating an album about herself, wanted to show how close she is to her father. "My mom gave me a ton of pictures from when I was little, and they're all in horrible construction paper albums and beginning to fade. I'm trying to incorporate them onto my layouts—almost then and now comparison layouts," she says. Marla chose this feature as the perfect setting for photos with her dad. She embellished the layout with contemporary colors, large monograms and repeating shapes.

Marla Kress, Cheswick, Pennsylvania

Supplies: Patterned paper, letter stickers (American Crafts); monogram letters (My Mind's Eye); rub-on words, woven label (Making Memories); circle punch (EK Success); cocoa, tan, white, blue and pink cardstocks; circle punch; ribbons; staples

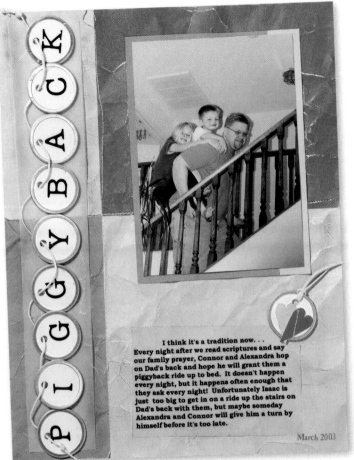

piggyback

Nighttime rituals can sneak up on a family. Like when MaryAnn's husband air-mailed two of their kids to bed via piggyback. Suddenly a new tradition was born. MaryAnn's journaling recounts that it "doesn't happen every night but it happens often enough that they ask every night!" Her page is a simple construction of patterned paper, circle metal-rimmed tags, vellum and chalking for an easygoing, graphic look.

MaryAnn Metcalf, Mesa, Arizona

Supplies: Color blocked paper (American Crafts); metal tag, date stamp (Making Memories); letter stickers, metal-rimmed tags (EK Success); metallic rub-ons (Craf-T); heart punch (Emagination Crafts); vellum; white jute

I think it's a tradition now. . . Every night after we read scriptures and say our family prayer, Connor and Alexandra hop on Dad's back and hope he will grant them a piggyback ride up to bed. It doesn't happen every night, but it happens often enough that they ask every night! Unfortunately Isaac is just too big to get in on a ride up the stairs on Dad's back with them, but maybe someday Alexandra and Connor will give him a turn by himself before it's too late.

March 2003

just me and my daddy

The transition from having one child to having another is sometimes dramatic. As Kelly approached this transition, she experienced nostalgia over the birth of her first child. Her journaling reflects the melancholy and the joy of becoming parents. "It was a bit more gradual for me," she says, "but for my husband, it was a definite moment—a true instant—where he felt he was suddenly a father, not just a father, but a daddy." Kelly's page elements reflect the natural feel of the park they visited that day and emphasize the daddy theme.

Kelly Goree, Shelbyville, Kentucky

Supplies: Patterned papers (Karen Foster Design, Pebbles); phrase stickers (EK Success); label maker (Dymo); stencil letters (Avery); ribbon (Michaels); jewelry tags, letter stamps (Making Memories); brown stamping ink; copper snap

eye 2 eye

Dar takes her camera everywhere, and once as she and her family waited for a car wash, her son hopped up on a bench to see if he could be as tall as his dad. When she got the photos back, she was struck by seeing their heads together. "Father and son, so different, yet so alike. Two people who constantly butt heads but have an unshakable bond and love each other without measure," she says. To give herself plenty of space to journal the story and her feelings about it, she included a tag book.

Dar Kaso, Virginia Beach, Virginia

Supplies: Patterned papers, tag book (K & Company); letter punches (EK Success); circle cutter (Provo Craft); rub-on letters (Making Memories); corner rounder (Creative Memories); blue, celery and cream cardstocks; circle cutter; twine; black pen; white gel pen; black stamping ink

ironman

Michelle's brother competed in an Ironman competition. "He was expecting his first child the following month," she says, "I wanted to convey my awe of him, of his gentle strength that makes him both a great athlete and a great dad. She kept the design simple to focus attention on the photos that showing the two worlds that Michelle spoke about.

Michelle Livingston, Centennial, Colorado
Ironman Photo: Action Sports International,
Tucker, Georgia

Supplies: Patterned papers (Anna Griffin, Chatterbox, Creative Imaginations, Daisy D's); journaling transparency (Scrapping With Style); distress ink (Ranger); acrylic letter stickers (Colorbök); label maker (Dymo); cream paper

my favorite place

Ellen's page of snapshots of her husband and daughter came to be when Ellen asked her husband to journal. "I sat him down at the dining room table one night after the kids had gone to bed and used my teacher voice on him." She also provided him support by being his secretary, recording his thoughts on paper. The design came together after Ellen purchased her first bunch of fibers. She used them with flair, choosing monochromatic tones and concentrating them in areas of importance.

Ellen Hargrove, Jenks, Oklahoma

Supplies: Patterned paper (K & Company); journaling pocket (Autumn Leaves); ribbons (EK Success, Making Memories); letter buttons (Junkitz); letter stamps (Hero Arts); cream and putty cardstocks; chalk; black pen; brown stamping ink

Daddy & Mary Catherine - Spring 2003

Your love for each other does not need words or memories. It has always been

. . . ten thousand words

LeeAndra lives several hours from her stepdaughters, so it makes the time they spend together more precious. She says, "I created this layout to showcase the love that is always there, despite how much time may pass between visits. It doesn't need verbal expression to make itself known." In order to enhance this theme on this digital layout, she added word art to a tender photo. She duplicated a small portion of the photo, framed it to give it emphasis and added it to the lower portion of the page with a small journaling block.

LeeAndra Slatten, Indianapolis, Indiana

Supplies: Image-editing software (Adobe Photoshop); photo filter (downloaded from the Internet)

daddy's girl

While celebrating Canada Day, Jennifer's daughter crawled up on her daddy's lap to snuggle. "That is when I got this precious photo," she says. Her inspiration for the page design came from the scrapbooking fabric. She used its colors throughout the layout, adding papers and ribbons to match.

Jennifer Johner, Asquith, Saskatchewan, Canada

Supplies: Striped fabric, word buttons (Junkitz); patterned paper (7 Gypsies); ribbons (Making Memories, Offray); letter stamps, rub-on letters (Making Memories); royal blue, white and red cardstocks (Bazzill); powder blue cardstock; black stamping ink; stencil letter

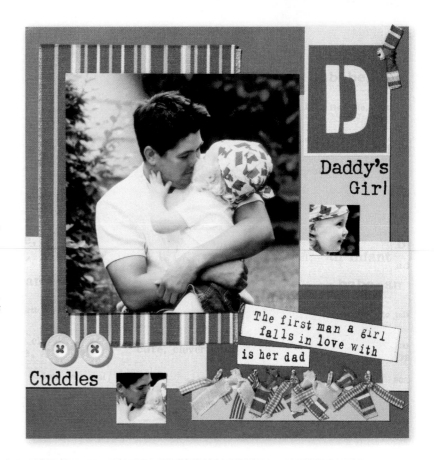

perfect start

After selling a rental house they had owned for 12 years, Stacy and her family took the trip they had promised themselves. She watched her daughters and husband, who love animals, wait silently by the water for the birds to come to them. The moment, she says, "had to be captured." Along with her action-packed photos, Stacy used strips of pre-torn fabric and wrapped them around cardstock strips. She liked the way the torn edges added softness to the page.

Stacy Yoder, Yucaipa, California

Supplies: Mat board frame (Savage Universal Corporation); torn fabric strips (Homemade Memories); tan and white cardstocks

My two kids!

Sometimes I think Steve is reliving his childhood moments through the fun times we have with our daughter Kiersten! It feels like I have two kids sometimes and I absolutely love that! Whether it is sliding down a snowy hill, tickle battles, or just a fun afternoon spent together, the two of them are always laughing and having fun. They have such a close relationship that I know will stand the test of time. I hope my two kids always have a heart that knows how to laugh and remember the carefree days of childhood.

Steve AND Kiersten

my two kids

The snow doesn't fly often in western North Carolina, but when it does, it brings delight. Heather's family took advantage of the slight accumulation to use their sled and take some photos. "Steve and Kiersten had so much fun," Heather says. "As I stood taking pictures of them and listening to them laugh, I couldn't help but think that they were 'my two kids'!" Heather surrounded her black-and-white photos with papers and embellishments in pale pink and green.

Heather Preckel, Swannanoa, North Carolina

Supplies: Patterned papers, cards, frames, letter stickers (Chatterbox); circle punch (Creative Memories); buttons (Junkitz); ribbons (Offray); label maker (Dymo); black and green cardstocks; sandpaper

paradise

Paradise is only a few hours away from home according to Maria and her family. They make time to travel to Clear Lake in Manitoba, Canada, nearly every year. One day, while her daughter combed the beach for treasures to give her dad, Maria snapped some photos. After choosing her favorites, she designed the layout by choosing "some bright striped paper to add punch and small embellishments to spice it up, while still keeping it simple."

Maria Burke, Steinbach, Manitoba, Canada

Supplies: Patterned paper, black flower (KI Memories); definition sticker, "dad" tag (Making Memories); ribbon (Offray); date stamp (Office Depot); white and navy cardstocks; red mulberry paper; brads; black stamping ink

SEP 1 8 2004

[par·a·dise]
perfection of beauty and peace

dad

We all had such a fun time playing at Clear Lake!

We spent the day stomping in the sand and throwing rocks into the lake.

One of Sarah's favorite things was finding treasures to show Daddy!

There's just something so magical about being at the beach.

just like papa

When Noah began playing with his dad's stethoscope, Bela says, "I took the opportunity and put on the surgeon's cap and shot a few photos." This impromptu photo shoot inspired her to journal about what he might be when he grows up. For her layout, Bela found papers and embellishments that coordinated with the colors in the photo and used a simple design to let the focal photo shine.

Bela Luis, Winnipeg, Manitoba, Canada

Supplies: Patterned papers, tabs, tags, acrylic circles, letter stickers (KI Memories); green cardstock (Bazzill); staples, black pen

that's my dad

Donna's father moved to sunny Florida after her mom died. She finds it difficult to be far away but treasures the time they do spend together. At a recent family party, she says, "We were all talking and I just kept taking pictures." Donna wanted to use all the best snapshots of her dad but felt it would make her page too busy. She enlarged one photo and hid the rest of the photos and her journaling under a flap. "I loved these papers and how I was able to match up the wording with the different colors," Donna says.

Donna Garza, Romeoville, Illinois

Supplies: Patterned papers (Mustard Moon); red ribbon, black tile, mini bottle cap letters (Li'l Davis Designs); hinges, label holder, washer, decorative brad, foam letter stamps (Making Memories); numbers stamps (source unknown); photo corners (Canson); black stamping ink; black acrylic paint; buckle; black cardstock; brads; elastic band

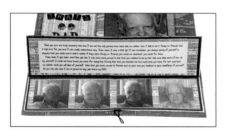

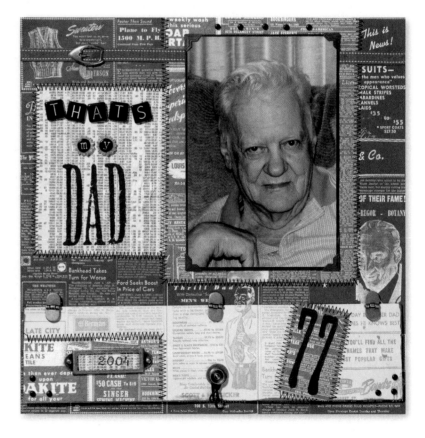

thank you daddy

While visiting Turkey Run State Park, Erin walked behind her husband and daughter, Abigail. "There was a tug on my heart watching them together. There he was already guiding her in the direction that she needs to go. He is her strength and her guide in so many ways," she says. Erin enjoys creating layouts from the perspective of her daughter and highlights things Abigail will value when she looks back later in life. This digital layout features a background of enlarged leaves with rich fall colors, echoing the photo's natural elements.

Erin Cassell, Indianapolis, Indiana

Supplies: Nature Thankful Kit by Anna Aspnes (www.scrapbook-elements.com); image-editing software (Adobe Photoshop 7.0)

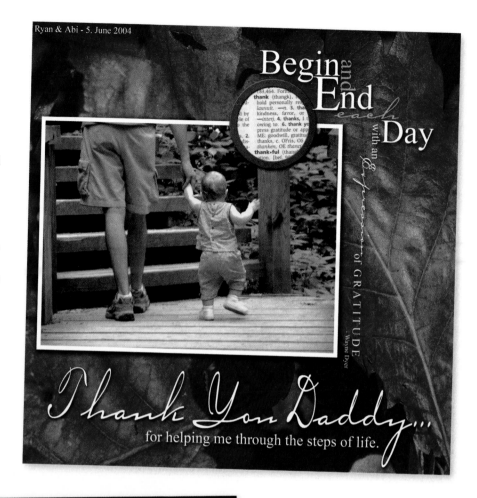

Ryan & Abi - 5. June 2004

Begin and End each Day with an expression of GRATITUDE - Wayne Dyer

Thank You Daddy...
for helping me through the steps of life.

ralph m. green

Susan's father, Ralph M. Green, lived his life behind a camera. When she began scrapbooking, she gained a new appreciation of his contribution to the family because of this passion. "I felt so fortunate to have these images of the past. It has made me realize the importance of recording the events of my own children's and grandchildren's lives in a permanent way," she says. "So, this all started with my dad, Ralph Green, and his love for us." Using self-portraits from her father, Susan designed a page featuring her journaling about his contribution to the family.

Susan Steffens, DeWitt, Michigan

Supplies: Image-editing software (Microsoft Digital Image Pro 9.0, Microsoft WordPerfect)

Ralph M. Green...The Man Behind the Camera

One afternoon while working on this scrapbook of family pictures taken many years ago by my dad, I started looking at them differently. I thought about my dad and how he must have felt as he was taking those pictures. After all, there's a lot of love that goes into wanting to preserve a memory of a person who will never, ever look that same way again. And, that time will pass away never to be seen again without the legacy of pictures.

Every time we take out our camera and shoot the tender, silly, wonderful moments in our lives we keep a visual history of them.

When we look at pictures of the past, we should see not only the person or place being immortalized, we should also think of the person behind the camera who loved us enough to want to save, forever, the special moments and feelings in those pictures. Maybe they aren't all photographic masterpieces, but they tell a story and keep people with us long after they are gone except in memories. Every one of the pictures I've included in this scrapbook was a special time and place both to the person in the picture and the person standing behind the camera.

Dad took so many pictures of us when we were kids that we just got used to seeing him with his camera in his hand. Until I started working on this scrapbook, I never thought too much about why he took them. Now, being the person with the camera in her hand, I realize that there is a good deal of love behind the desire to capture a fleeting, happy memory.

Dad always told us that a person is never truly gone until the last person who knew him is gone too. With pictures, we help keep those memories alive for people who come after us. Look at these pictures as more than just a cute or pretty shot of a person or place...they are small capsules of a time that meant something to both the person in the picture and the person taking it..

My Dad
1913 - 1997

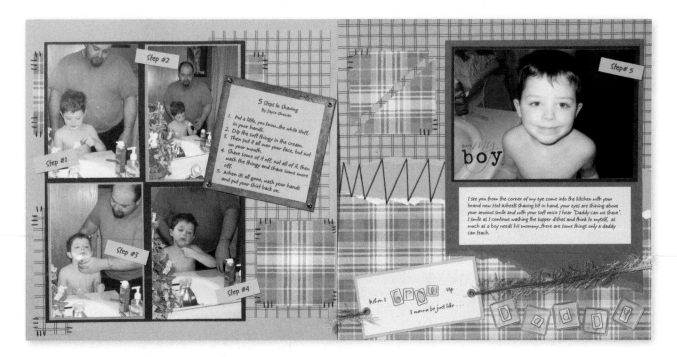

when i grow up

One of life's rites of passage for a boy is learning to shave with daddy. Aimee created this page to demonstrate the process. "To sweeten the layout, I thought it would be adorable to have my son describe the steps," she says. She recorded verbatim what he said and used a journaling block with step numbers to coincide with the photos. Aimee sewed touches of fibers to the page to give it a warm and welcoming feel.

Aimee Grenier, Hinton, Alberta, Canada

Supplies: Patterned papers (Mustard Moon); letter stickers (Doodlebug Design): journaling sticker (Creative Imaginations); metal-rimmed vellum tags (Making Memories); spring green, evergreen, tan and putty cardstocks; silver brads; green eyelets; fibers; walnut ink; brown embroidery floss

thankful

While at her family reunion, Leah caught a glimpse of her husband and son playing. As she watched them together, she was reminded of how much she appreciates their love for each other. She journaled her thoughts and feelings about that moment. Leah completed this page at a crop and says, "I already had the basics of the journaling in my head, so it was no problem putting the page together among the distractions of the room full of fellow scrappers."

Leah LaMontagne, Las Vegas, Nevada

Supplies: Patterned papers (Carolee's Creations, C-Thru Ruler); mini stamps, letter stamps (Hero Arts); letter stickers (EK Success); black stamping ink; tan, cream, blue and brown cardstocks; ribbons

my family

Like many scrapbookers, Heather feels that sometimes her camera is permanently attached to her, but it definitely pays off. She took these candid photos of her husband and daughter while they played outside. Her hinged photo, when opened, reveals another pose featuring silly faces. Heather wanted to use both photos, but not adjacent to each other. She says her design highlights that "there are two sides to people. What you see on the outside may not always be what you see on the inside."

Heather Preckel, Swannanoa, North Carolina

Supplies: Patterned papers, definition twill (7 Gypsies); label maker (Dymo); walnut ink (Postmodern Design); heart punch (Emagination Crafts); black photo corners (3M); rub-on quote, brads (Making Memories); black stamping ink; black and white cardstocks; gold hinges

alex and dad

Susan loves designing pages with texture. The tassels and fibers on this page coordinate with the warm, homey feeling in the photos. The journaling came after she hatched a little plan for her husband. "I actually created the page first and showed it to him, he made a couple of comments and I asked if he would type it into the computer so I could use it for the journaling. You can definitely see my husband's character in the journaling."

Susan Stringfellow, Cypress, Texas

Supplies: Patterned papers (K & Company, Paper Loft); embossed vellum (K & Company); foam letter stamps (Making Memories); fibers (Fibers By The Yard); tassel trim (Wrights); green and gold acrylic paints; red and sage cardstocks; gold brads; transparency

true treasure

Beachcombing is one of Lisa and her family's favorite activities. They hunt for treasures, explore, play and enjoy each other's company. As she designed a beach layout of their trip to Hatteras, North Carolina, she says, "I looked at this photo and all I could think was that these guys are my true treasures. I decided to pull the photo out and do a separate layout." She created a simple design using a pair of premade embellishments, a quadruple-matted photo and a touch of handwritten journaling.

Lisa Turley, Chesapeake, Virginia

Supplies: Patterned paper (7 Gypsies); letter stickers, buckle (Making Memories); heart stickers, key and heart embellishment (EK Success); black organza ribbon (Offray); black, red and white cardstocks (Bazzill); black pen; chalk; silver brads and eyelets

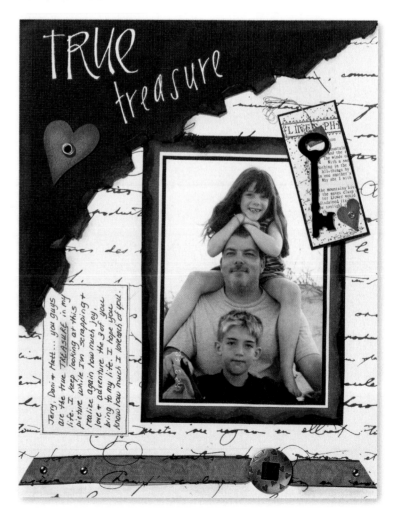

swimming with dad

Michele says, "I had several shots of the kids playing in the kiddie pool, but when my husband got in with them, I knew I needed a shot of that, too!" To preserve the memory of that day, she created a layout highlighting her favorite photo. She embellished the page with a coordinating line of paper elements, including borders, cut-out embellishments and a tag.

Michele Hamby, Guthrie, Oklahoma

Supplies: Patterned papers, die cuts, tag (Outdoors & More Scrapbook Decor); ribbon (Michaels); letter stickers (Creative Imaginations); yellow cardstock (Bazzill); black pen; brown stamping ink

my girl

Vacations of rest and relaxation aren't always fun for little ones. They want action. Shaunte's daughter, Mikayla, got antsy, so Daddy took her for a walk. Shaunte says, "I remember how sweet they looked, her so little and newly walking, and Sam so patient, letting her walk at her own clumsy pace." While completing the page, Shaunte asked her husband to journal. She says, "It was like he remembered that day too and knew exactly what he wanted to say." She chose papers to echo the photograph colors, crumpled other paper for texture and used paint to embellish metal elements.

Shaunte Wadley, Lehi, Utah

Supplies: Patterned papers (Chatterbox); vellum (Provo Craft); photo turns (7 Gypsies); metal frame, metal eyelet letters (Making Memories); triangular conchos (www.memoriesoftherabbit.com); ribbon; silver brads; red acrylic paint

dad and me

Tracy received a 35mm, completely manual camera for Christmas and learned to use it while spending time with her family. She says they get "impatient while they wait posed for the sound of the shutter, but after a while of waiting, real life resumes." That's when she captures her favorite moments. Tracy loves using symbols on her pages. For this one, she says, "The nuts, wire and washers are symbols of a father, and the ribbon, a symbol of a little girl. The puzzle pieces symbolize our family as a close unit."

Tracy Austin, Bossier City, Louisiana

Supplies: Patterned paper (Paper Company); ribbons (Bobbin Robin); rub-on words (Making Memories); "&" sticker (EK Success); wire easel spiral (7 Gypsies); acrylic label holder (KI Memories); corner rounder (Marvy); silver brads; washers and nuts; black pen

who, what, when, where, why

Action shots play an important role in scrapbooks. They show the importance of family time and will bring special memories when grown children revisit the albums. Summer took these photos of her husband with their sons during a "tickle fest." She says, "I created the page using a funky retro style and converted the photos to sepia to keep the focus on the photos and not the distracting colors or clothing in the photos." To personalize slide mounts, she covered them with coordinating papers.

Summer Ford, Bulverde, Texas

Supplies: Patterned papers (Chatterbox); foam flower stamp (Making Memories); printed twill (7 Gypsies); plain twill (Great Balls of Fiber); twill letter tabs (Carolee's Creations); slide mounts (Magic Scraps); letter stamps (Hero Arts, Stampin'Up!); black stamping ink; red embroidery floss; cream cardstock; distress ink; acyrlic paints

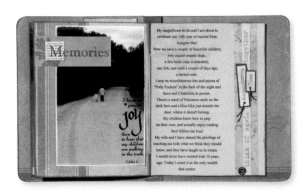

family man

Angie created a mini album honoring her husband and the exceptional father he is to their two children. She expresses her gratitude for his commitment to his family's walk of faith. Angie says, "Your love for us is faithful and strong, it sustains us and we thrive as a family because of it." For the journaling, Angie used her husband's own words from letters he's written and stories he's told. Papers rich in brown, suede and beige complement the album's masculine theme.

Angie Head, Friendswood, Texas

Supplies: Album (Halcraft); patterned papers (Crossed Paths); ledger paper, chipboard letters (Making Memories); rub-on word (Li'l Davis Designs); ribbon (May Arts); photo corners (Karen Foster Design); file folder (Autumn Leaves); zipper pull (All My Memories); elastic band closures (7 Gypsies); chalk ink (Clearsnap); word stickers (Crossed Paths, Making Memories, Pebbles); suede spray paint (Krylon)

immediate family

CHAPTER THREE

Every family has its own story. Mothers, fathers, brothers, sisters, step-siblings, stepparents and even pets share in the creation of each family's story. In families we take turns doing chores, laugh together while watching our favorite TV shows and share our hopes and dreams. With all its beliefs, all its weaknesses and all its strengths, the family is truly life's greatest blessing.

It's no wonder that the faces of family members most often grace the pages of scrapbooks. From everyday moments at the dinner table to special occasions celebrating a graduation or birth of a child, our family is our heartbeat. So capture each precious moment and engrave its place in time through everlasting scrapbook pages.

When we were first married, Trace and I couldn't imagine loving another being more than our dog. Four kids later, we love being parents and can't imagine why we waited so long for the experience!

—*Denise Tucker*

"The family
is one of nature's masterpieces."

—George Santayana

Just the two of us...that was the framework of our family for more than six years after we said, "I do." The throw-sized quilt we created as a couple seemed adequate. We completed each other, yet eventually we had a desire to share our love with a little one.

Along came Trent in 1990 and our quilt now fit a twin-sized bed. It was a charming family, consisting of two parents who doted profusely on their first-born son.

Three years later, to the day, Tanner joined our family, and our quilt and hearts miraculously extended to full-size. He wove new fabrics into this creation. His threads were different shades than Trent's, yet in many ways they appeared so similar and blended flawlessly.

Health issues indicated that our quilt should not be expanded; yet in 1997, Ty again enlarged our Tucker quilt. We were queen-sized now, and I was the queen reigning in a home of males. Our quilt was warm and cozy, and we couldn't imagine it growing any larger.

However, God knew that his handiwork was not yet finished. He wanted us to bridge the expanse of a king-sized bed. He also wanted us to admire and appreciate the beautiful fabrics and textures a little girl could contribute to this quilt, so in 1999, Toria became the exquisite appliqué on our ever-enlarging quilt.

In less than ten years, our family had grown from two to six, and it now seems difficult to fathom our quilt even a fraction of an inch smaller than its current size. We are a seamless family now...stitched together with love and woven to completion.

i remember

Nicole created a "collage of memories" on this page from e-mail questions she sent to her siblings over the course of a year. They copied the messages to one another to help jog more memories. "I then compiled the e-mails and printed them out," she says. "This page led to a mini album that I made each sibling and my mom for Christmas." With so many important elements, Nicole shuffled them around on the spread until she liked the look.

Nicole Keller, Rio Hondo, Texas

Supplies: Patterned papers (Bo-Bunny Press, Karen Foster Design, Provo Craft); letter stickers (Wordsworth); flower and striped punch-outs (KI Memories); flower charms (Paper Connection); paper flowers, photo turns, black ribbon, date stamp (Making Memories); flower and gingham ribbon (Offray); vellum envelopes (EK Success); pink and white cardstocks (Bazzill); pink paint; red, orange, black and pink brads; staples; black pen

a family stitched with love

Debbie's family roots run deep in Twisp, Washington, where her husband's grandfather helped build the town. While Debbie and her family attended this grandfather's funeral, the hotel where they stayed displayed the tractor in the photos. "My hubby mentioned that his grandpa could have even driven it so many years ago. I just thought it was appropriate that we take a bit of history . . . back with us." Debbie symbolized her feelings that Grandpa was "the thread that held the whole family together" by using sewing box papers and embellishments in her design.

Debbie Weller, Kalispell, Montana

Supplies: Patterned papers, vellum, coin holders, index tab, needle holder stencil, word twist ties, file folder (Club Scrap); letter stamps (Lost Coast Designs, Sunday International); foam letter stamps (found at local dollar store); metal latch (7 Gypsies); love definition stamp (Lost Coast Designs); square paper clips (Making Memories); label maker (Dymo); letter sticker (Provo Craft); blue, turquoise and red cardstocks; silver eyelets; blue embroidery floss; safety pins; eggplant and black stamping inks; black pen; white acrylic paint

I Thought

I thought it would matter that you were adopted. I thought it would bother me that I didn't have baby pictures. I thought that those 21 months you lived life before you reached my arms would always be a hole in my life. In your life. In our life together. I thought that adoption would prevent you from being the spittin' image of your dad. I thought we would never see those shared personality traits.

Adoption is an event that happens in a family—a one time occurrence. Life changing, yes, but it's not a life long condition. But being my son—THAT is a condition that means everything. You are my son and are all the world to me. I honestly forget about adoption and genetics and those months of your life before you reached us. I thought all those things would bother me.

I thought wrong.

W R O N G

i thought

Elizabeth's family adopted Guerby from Haiti when he was 21 months old. Her passion to love all her kids, to express her feelings about adoption and to help others understand the process, inspired this page. "It's a one-time event. Just like I don't think every day of the actual birth of my biological kids ... I don't think that one is adopted," she says. "It's a good reminder to me and to Guerby that life and love take over." Her colorful design of bright orange, green and blue highlights the happy faces of mother and son.

Elizabeth Ruuska, Rensselaer, Indiana

Supplies: Patterned papers (Basic Grey); mesh (Magic Mesh); black letter stickers (Doodlebug Design); zipper, acrylic circle, buckle, fabric (Junkitz); acrylic letter (Heidi Grace Designs); flower punch (EK Success); metal tag letters (Making Memories); zipper pull; orange and green cardstocks; orange and green ribbons; mini brads; turquoise paint; staple

special choice

The story of adoption varies from family to family. Amy shares her dramatic story in this page with an enlarged portrait and expansive journaling, recounting her daughter's story. A co-worker shared that she knew of a young woman who was 8 months' pregnant and wanted to give her baby up for adoption. Amy says, "At that very moment, my heart soared, and I think my feet came off the ground. Could this be the real thing? Or would this be another false start, leading to disappointment and despair yet again?"

Amy Goldstein, Kent Lakes, New York

Supplies: Patterned paper, transparency (Autumn Leaves); fleur-de-lis charm (EK Success); decorative metal brads (Making Memories)

Remembering the good times.

REMEMBER WHEN

Special Choice

Sometimes the ability to begin and continue a family is a choice that is taken for granted by many people ... Including our Family. After many years of false starts with the public adoption system, foster care and traditional adoptions, you came to us because of nothing more than the fate of being in the "right" place at the right time.

I had been working for a new company in Manhattan and was finally beginning to feel at home with the wonderful people that also worked there. One particular person seemed to have quite a bit to share with me and I felt at home talking with her. Carol was an administrative assistant in my department and, as luck would have it, was the person who had been assigned to support me.

Carol was an outgoing vivacious person that was always willing to share a humorous limerick or funny story and was always gabbing about something. One day, while trading anecdotes, I had told her our family's story of trying to adopt a baby with all of its heartbreak. She seemed to listen quietly and said nothing. I babbled on and gave her my entire life story and assumed that she must have thought I was a maniac for sharing all the intimate details of our struggle.

About a week later, Carol asked me if I wanted to take a walk and get a cup of coffee with her to which I said "Sure, I would love to!" As we rode done in the elevator, she inquired if we were still trying to adopt to which I replied "Yes, but I try not to get down about it." "Well, I know of a girl that is 8 months pregnant and wants to give the baby up for adoption and I would love to introduce you to her if you are still interested".

At that very moment, my heart soared and I think my feet came off the ground. Could this be the real thing??? Or would this be another false start leading to disappointment and despair yet again?

Well, the rest, as they say, is history!!! You have been a part of our family since the day you were born and you are OUR very own SPECIAL CHOICE!

LIFE ISN'T A MATTER OF *milestones–* BUT OF *moments.*

picture perfect family

While taking a monthlong graduate school exam, Lizzy missed time to celebrate her engagement and her brother's graduation from college. After she successfully passed her exam, her mom planned a celebration in San Francisco. While touring near the Golden Gate Bridge, she says, "A nice German tourist approached us to ask if we'd like to get our picture taken. As it turns out, it's the only picture of the four of us from that trip." It became her favorite, so she used it several times on her page, reducing the image and applying several filters in image-editing software.

Lizzy Mayorga, Seattle, Washington

Supplies: Patterned papers, canvas quote (Chatterbox); metal-rimmed tag (Avery); stencil letter (Target); letter stickers (DieCuts with a View); blue and tan cardstocks (Bazzill); large jump ring; fibers; black pen; black stamping ink

Picture Perfect **FAMILY**

Happy people are the fizz in the soda of life.
-Anonymous

I simply love this picture of the four of us together. It really brings across our love for each other and our ease around each other. We may bicker & get on each other's nerves, as every family does... but we love to be together, joking, laughing, seeing the world. I am so happy that Jorgito & Mom love Mike as much as they do. "I'm so excited to have a new son," Mami said to him on this trip. I love all three of them so much!

a happy family

Ellen set up for their annual Christmas card photo shoot. She set up the camera and tripod and had a friend stand in for her while she got everything prepared. They switched places and her friend took several shots. She featured this captivating photo using earthy colored papers, fibers and stickers. Her hidden journaling accentuates the photo's theme by recounting her youthful dreams of how Ellen imagined the perfect family. For each dream, she replied to how life really is. She has found it to be different but full and lovely.

Ellen Hargrove, Jenks, Oklahoma

Supplies: Letter stickers (Creative Imaginations); letter and number stamps (Hero Arts, Wordsworth); fibers (Timeless Touches); label holder (Li'l Davis Designs); olive and tan cardstocks; vellum; brads; black pen; staples; chalks; black stamping ink

a happy FAMILY 2003 lift

we are family

It only takes a second to imagine what inspired Natalie's page. Natalie confirms, "I was going for a 'Brady Bunch' feel to this layout by having the four of us appear to be looking at each other in the photos." Each person photographed wore a white shirt, allowing the retro papers to add punches of color and lots of style.

Natalie Quandt, Rochester, Minnesota

Supplies: Patterned papers, word stickers (SEI)

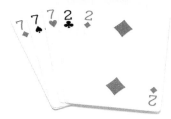

family

A day at the lake brings plenty of opportunity for a family photo shoot. Sherri created this page using two photos, and she journaled an inspirational message about ways their family lives together. It speaks of the pride that Sherri and her husband want to instill in their boys. The neutral tones, including black-and-white photos, letter stickers, stamped words and metal elements, give the page a cohesive look.

*Sherri Winstead, Fayetteville,
North Carolina*

Supplies: Patterned papers, letter stickers, word sticker, pewter ball chain, charm (Pebbles); letter stamps (Hero Arts); heart plaque and date stamp (Making Memories); letter stickers (Card Connection, Li'l Davis Designs, Wordsworth); scrabble letter (source unknown); black photo corners (Canson); tan and black cardstocks (Bazzill); unity tag (source unknown); copper brad; black and brown stamping inks

for love or money

Reality TV? No, it's real life. Stacy's journaling recounts that her husband had the opportunity to apply for a new job with more money but more work. Together they weighed the options before he was to attend a hiring session. She says, "He struggled to decide whether future financial security and the opportunities that could come with it would be better in the long run for us." Her husband made a decision and said "I choose love." The family celebrated the decision with a day of fun together.

Stacy Yoder, Yucaipa, California

Supplies: Ribbon (Offray); letter stamps (Ma Vinci's Reliquary, PSX Design); acrylic frame and hearts (Heidi Grace Designs); tan and cream acrylic paints; sage, cocoa, pink and cream cardstocks; brown and black stamping inks; clear embossing powder; chalk

our family

After Terri's sister took photos of her in-laws' 40th anniversary reunion, she went to Terri's house to do a portrait of Terri's immediate family. Terri created this page while taking part in a local stash challenge to include altered letters. Terri matted the photo, created the title and then realized the cardstock was too plain. By printing meaningful words and events onto cardstock, she created her own background paper.

Terri Davenport, Toledo, Ohio
Photo: Theresa Board, Gilbert, Arizona

Supplies: Label maker sticker (Pebbles); acrylic letter (KI Memories); letter stamp (Hero Arts); metal letter, rub-on letters, metal-rimmed tag (Making Memories); black concho (Scrapworks); letter brad (Jo-Ann Stores); navy and powder blue cardstocks; twill tape; black stamping ink

two of my favorite people

While Samuel visited his parents' winter home in Yuma, Arizona, they all attended a craft fair where they took this photo. When Samuel designed the page, the story of his 16th birthday kept coming to mind as an example of the love his parents have continually shown him. To create the title, he says, "I used different fonts, sticker letters, wood tile letters, etc., to reflect the many ways in which we show and reflect the love we have for one another." Desert colors prevailed in this layout, representing Arizona.

Samuel Cole, Stillwater, Minnesota

Supplies: Patterned paper (NRN Designs); die-cut letters (QuicKutz); costal netting (Jest Charming); wooden letter tiles (source unknown); letter stamps (Hero Arts, PSX Design); cancellation stamp (American Stamps); page pebble, decorative brads (Making Memories); angel stamp (Comotion Rubber Stamps); terra cotta and sage cardstocks; black stamping ink; dark moss, amber clay and yellow citrus chalk inks; black pen

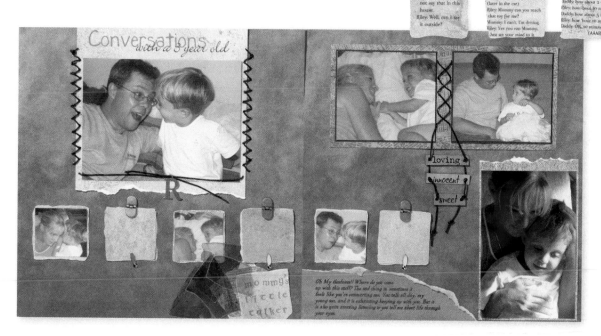

conversations with a 3-year-old

There comes a time in many parents' lives when a child's logic skills seem to push the envelope of social mores. "Shut up!" said Holly's son, to which she replied, "We don't say that in this house." "Well, can I say it outside?" Holly documented this amusing and sometimes frustrating time with her witty little one. She took photos of their conversations and wrote the anecdotes on journaling boxes, hidden under hinged covers. She embellished the spread with mica, cording and metal elements.

Holly Pittroff, Huntersville, North Carolina

Supplies: Patterned papers (Cloud 9 Design, Karen Foster Design, Rusty Pickle); waxed black twine (Pepperell Braiding); letter charm, photo flips (Making Memories); photo turns (7 Gypsies); mica (USArtQuest); letter stamps (PSX Design); metal word charms (DieCuts with a View); crystal lacquer (Sakura Hobby Craft); silver brads; chalk; brown stamping ink

life . . . without sisters

This photo, taken while Susan and her sisters were together for Christmas in 2004, demonstrates the love and care they have for one another. She says, "I looked at this picture and was instantly reminded of how much fun I always have with my sisters. That led me to think about how greatly my sisters have shaped my life." She filled her layout with delightfully feminine touches of pink and brown, soft flowers, ribbons and vintage buttons.

Susan Weinroth, Centerville, Minnesota

Supplies: Patterned paper (American Crafts); faux brown leather paper (FiberMark); acrylic letters, flower (KI Memories); wooden letters (Li'l Davis Designs); letter stamps (PSX Design); ribbons (Creative Imaginations, May Arts); canvas fabric; pink cardstock; silk flowers, green and brown brads; buttons; black stamping ink

sister like you

The natural light in Susan's apartment made it a perfect setting for this photo shoot with her sister. She used her tripod and timer to achieve this professional-style snapshot. Susan designed the feminine page with bright colors and soft ribbons to contrast with the black-and-white photo. She says, "I wanted the word 'sister' to stand out on the page, so I stamped each letter onto cardstock and trimmed them separately."

Susan Weinroth, Centerville, Minnesota

Supplies: Patterned papers, paint chip (SEI); rub-on letters (Doodlebug Design, Scrapworks); letter stamps (Ma Vinci's Reliquary); turquoise and purple cardstocks (Bazzill); ribbons; white stamping ink; purple brad

and they called us JJ[4]

Janetta's family is close, due in part to the inspiration of her father who instilled in them an attitude that family comes first. She says, "Growing up, we weren't just brothers and sisters, but also friends. I remember during high school, I was always with a sibling and unlike my friends who thought acknowledging or talking to a sibling was embarrassing or 'taboo,' I loved it." Each sibling is named with the first and middle initials "J," so thier dad gave each a double syllable nickname—J.J., Jo-Jo, Jan-Jan and Jun-Jun. Janetta highlights this special memory in her retro-themed design.

Janetta Abucejo Wieneke, Memory Makers Books
Photos: John G. Abucejo

Supplies: Patterned papers (Sassafras Lass); copper oval paper clips (Nunn Design); chipboard stencil letters (Making Memories); die-cut number (DMD); word stamp (PSX Design); clear circular frame (Scrapworks); woven label (Junkitz); label maker (Dymo); gold photo corners (Canson); square punch (EK Success); black cardstock; brads; brown stamping ink; blue and brown acrylic paint

my big sister

Little ones can't fully comprehend what a baby in Mommy's tummy will finally mean, but meeting the sibling for the first time is a joyous occasion. Jonah created this page so "Christian, my son, would know his big sister loved him from the moment they met, and to remind me that their relationship is not just one of blood but of love and affection." She chose soft reds to communicate love, to enhance her daughter's clothing and to give a sweet look to this page featuring her newborn.

Jonah Toleno, Glendale, Arizona

Supplies: Patterned papers (Basic Grey, Creative Imaginations); foam letter stamps, leather flower, label holder (Making Memories); printed transparency (Daisy D's); printed twill (7 Gypsies); black pen; black brads; black chalk ink; orange and yellow acrylic paints

named with love

Naming a child is one of the greatest joys and challenges of expectant parents. Summer recorded the reasons she and her husband chose each child's name. She says, "So many people ask about them, and I figured it was definitely scrapbook worthy! I used photos I already had and just converted them to black-and-white." Summer used neutral browns, creams and black page elements with silver accents to give the page a classic heritage feel.

Summer Ford, Bulverde, Texas

Supplies: Patterned papers (Frances Meyer, K & Company, Provo Craft); letter stamps (Stampin' Up!); metal letter charms, photo corners, date stamp, heart charm (Making Memories); label holder (Jo-Ann Stores); organza ribbon (Offray); fiber (Lion Brand); buttons; black embroidery floss; black cardstock; flat head eyelets; black embossing powder; black stamping ink; sandpaper

play together

Lisa's family enjoys their huge backyard, and the kids often play there. This day they focused their attention for hours on one project and worked together to complete it. Lisa says, "It was just a 'normal' day which is what made these photos so special for me. I was thrilled to see how well they came out, and I wanted to create a fun layout for them to remember the day." She used bright spring colors for her papers and paint to bring out the fun and youthful theme of the page.

Lisa Turley, Chesapeake, Virginia

Supplies: Patterned paper (Karen Foster Design); die-cut title (Sarah Heidt Photo Craft); canvas phrase and tag, round clay word, library pocket (Li'l Davis Designs); rub-on letters (Autumn Leaves); safety pins, sage, off white and black cardstocks (Bazzill); gingham ribbon; mini brads; acrylic paint; black pen

big sister, li'l brother

Sherry's stepdaughter and son don't get much time to spend together, so when they are together she takes plenty of photos. "I want them to have lots of photos to remember their times together," she says. "My journaling reflects how I feel about their relationship and that someday, when they look at these pages, they will realize how important family is." To coordinate the background, photos and the subjects' clothing, Sherry used earth-toned papers and embellishments.

Sherry Wright, West Branch, Michigan

Supplies: Patterned papers, letter stickers (Arctic Frog); metal words (Making Memories); ribbons (Me & My Big Ideas); brown stamping ink; tan and green cardstocks; transparency; burlap; acrylic paints

waking up . . .

Sharon's son, Jonathan, needs a bit of snuggle time every morning to help him wake up. This particular morning, Brittany, his big sister, happened to be the recipient. Sharon says, "Jonathan crawled into her lap and they snuggled. It took about 15 minutes before he was ready to jump down and start the day. I snapped a few pictures, trying to capture this morning ritual." She kept the spread monochromatic in pink hues accented with the black-and-white photos, fibers and buttons.

Sharon Laakkonen, Superior, Wisconsin

Supplies: Patterned papers (Creative Imaginations); printed transparency, fibers (Scrapping With Style); square punches (Creative Memories); pink buttons, acrylic charm (Doodlebug Design); rub-on letters (Making Memories); acrylic hearts (Heidi Grace Designs); silver medallions (Card Connection); organza ribbon (Offray); pink and white cardstocks (Bazzill); white stamping ink; pink embroidery floss

i served the cake . . .

When Susan's sister was diagnosed with cancer a number of years ago, she wanted to create a gift for her to show her appreciation for all she had meant to her. "'I Served the Cake' was originally a group of pictures I framed and gave to my sister along with the poem that I used for journaling," she says. "I gave her the framed collage for her birthday the year she passed away." When she began a scrapbook about her children's heritage, she wanted them to meet their aunt and she created this page, inspired by the original framed piece.

Susan Steffens, DeWitt, Michigan

Supplies: Image-editing software (Microsoft Digital Image Pro 9.0, Microsoft WordPerfect)

brotherly love

While Sharon's sons played baseball, she says, "Every time Jonathan would 'catch' the ball, he would run back to Brayden and give him a big hug. Brayden is proud of being the 'big brother' and is always a willing recipient to Jonathan's affections." This baseball game inspired Sharon to choose the diamond fabric. To print journaling on it, she recommends attaching it to cardstock and setting the printer for thick paper. To finish the title, Sharon trimmed four triangles and applied a rub-on letter to each.

Sharon Laakkonen, Superior, Wisconsin

Supplies: Patterned paper (Me & My Big Ideas); printed transparency (Sweetwater); rub-on letters (Making Memories); black solvent stamping ink (Tsukineko); brown stamping ink; green, navy and black cardstocks; black brads

the art of being . . .

It is a rare pleasure to capture such a stunning moment of children playing as the sun sets. Sande enhanced the moment by using warm tones in her papers, featuring a large focal photo. She printed the photo twice and tore the border of one to adhere on top as a frame. She says, "My main message with this layout was to convey to my sons that they never forget to enjoy the simple fun of running on the beach or playing in the sand." The torn edges, twine and metal embellishments complement the photo's natural beauty.

Sande Krieger, Salt Lake City, Utah

Supplies: Patterned paper (Carolee's Creations); image-editing software (Adobe Photoshop Creative Suite); boys definitions, transparency words (7 Gypsies); rub-on words (Making Memories); silver nailheads (American Tag Co.); watch crystal concho (Scrapworks); silver knocker (Nunn Design); brown stamping ink; red cardstock; silver brad; twine; black pen

coming soon

Waiting for a new member of the family fills the mind with anticipation, wonder and plenty of emotions. Jessie designed this page to express some of what she imagined her growing family would experience after the little one arrived. Her design includes delicately colored papers and embellishments highlighting a progression of up-close images. Jessie says, "I lined them up. I think it gave the sense of something approaching or impending, in this case, the birth."

Jessie Baldwin, Las Vegas, Nevada

Supplies: Patterned paper (Me & My Big Ideas); safety pin, jump ring (Making Memories); metal square charm (Pebbles); letter stickers (Creative Imaginations); transparency; sage cardstock; blue ribbon

true love

A simple event such as dinner out with family can turn into an enchanting page. One night after dinner at one of their favorite restaurants, Suzy noticed her parents' loving demeanor and asked to take their photo. "My dad grabbed my mom's hand and leaned into her. I love this picture of them," she says. Suzy created this page to honor her parents' enduring love. She chose sophisticated hues with romantic designs and embellishments and journaled about their example of true love.

Suzy West, Fremont, California

Supplies: Patterned paper (Daisy D's); square punch (Creative Memories); rub-on letters (EK Success); letter stickers (Me & My Big Ideas); metal molding (Making Memories); fibers; avocado and olive cardstocks; cream acrylic paint; transparency

family

Lisa proves in her mini album that there is no greater wealth than the love of family. She used a thank-you letter format for journaling in which she thanks each member of her immediate family for being in her life. She says, "The idea for a gratitude album came to me while reading a book called *Simple Abundance* by Sarah Ban Breathnach (Warner Books). It got me thinking how lucky I am to have my family. Each page highlights a character trait they possess which I admire." Letter beads, colorful fibers and chipboard letters add creative flair to each page.

Lisa Dixon, East Brunswick, New Jersey

Supplies: Album (K & Company); patterned papers, fibers (Basic Grey); ribbons (Making Memories); distress ink (Ranger); watermark ink (Tsukineko); letter beads, letter stamps (Nicole, Inc.); chipboard letters, words (Li'l Davis Designs); license plate (Sticker Studio); stick pins (EK Success); hook-and-eye fasteners (Prym-Dritz); gold embossing powder; transparency; cardstock

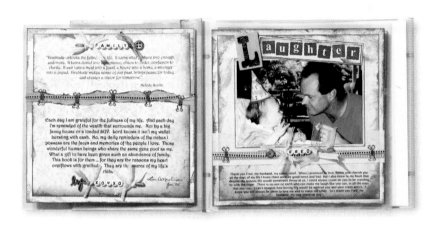

extended
family

CHAPTER FOUR

Family truly is the tie that binds. The stories and traditions that get passed from generation to generation are our links to our history and our heritage.

Each family member leaves their footprints in our memory with his or her unique personality and character. Grandma adds a sweet magic touch to all her meals, has a supply of candy that never seems to run out and loves us like no one else. Grandpa can fix anything, tells out-of-this-world stories and lets us break the rules when Grandma is not looking. Teasing aunts and uncles provide never-ending laughter with their silly jokes and facial expressions. Fun-loving cousins are the playmates we cavort with when creating a ruckus in our grandparents' back yard.

Scrapbook pages filled with photos of close relatives will take us on a walk through the fields of memory. Keep family memories alive with scrapbook pages that preserve cherished times with those you love most.

My Aunty Olwen was one of my favorite relatives. She always wrote letters that were so fun and creative. I will always look back with a smile as I remember her quirky gifts and colorful personality.

—*Trudy Sigurdson*

> "Call it a clan, call it a network, call it a tribe, call it a family. Whatever you call it, whoever you are, you need one."
>
> —Jane Howard, "Families"

OaT HaNGeRS &

COLOURING BOOKS

...nty Olwen is one of the ...colourful characters in ...mily and has given me ...of my fondest childhood ...ries.

...Mum and Dad would go ...for the evening or to ...e shows in London, Aunty ...n would often look after ...nd Steve and she usually ...e baring gifts. One time ...brought us coat hangers. ...ave no idea why she ...ght coat hangers would ...e the perfect gift for a 7 ...9 year old, but she did. ...now, years later, I don't ...ember what the other ...ts were (probably ...louring books and sweets), ...t I'll never forget the coat ...ngers. Photo - June 2002

AUNTY OLWEN AND TRUDY

family

Beginning with her parents' 25th wedding anniversary, Laurel and her extended family have gathered for a professional photo shoot every five years. This photo captures her parents' 45th anniversary. She says, "It's so interesting to look at these portraits done over the past 25 years and see how much our family changes." Marlene, the photographer, captures family interactions by telling them to chat with each other. "It's amazing how the closeness of our family so clearly shines through in the photo," Laurel says. Her design features warm papers, metal embellishments and a poem.

Laurel Moser, Steinbach, Manitoba, Canada
Photo: Marlene's Designer Portraits, Mitchell, Manitoba, Canada

Supplies: Patterned papers (7 Gypsies, Chatterbox, K & Company, PSX Design); definition twill (7 Gypsies); decorative brad, metal label holder, white photo turns, tag (Making Memories); mesh (Magenta); fiber (On The Surface); red, stone and black cardstocks; copper brads

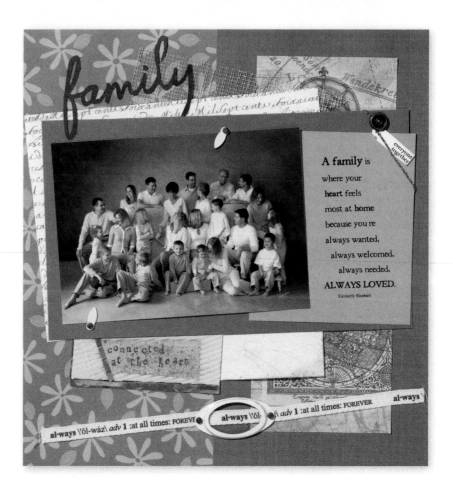

generations

Keeping the image of a fan in mind, Danielle created this family tree page for her son using photos and information from family members. Respecting original heritage photos, Danielle scanned them, printed them and returned them to the original owners. "I liked the idea of making it look like a quilt," she says. "I wanted this to have an old, antique look, like something you'd find in your grandmother's attic." Danielle accomplished this by using soft patterned papers in muted tones while incorporating patches of papers, machine stitching and homey embellishments.

Danielle Thompson, Tucker, Georgia

Supplies: Image-editing software (Adobe Photoshop); patterned papers (Anna Griffin, Basic Grey, Kopp Design); ribbon (Michaels); buttons (Junkitz, Wal-Mart); sequin flowers (Marcel Shurman); epoxy letter stickers (K & Company); brown cardstock; chalk; black pen

first family, now friends

Barb's journaling tells the story of growing up much older than her cousins. The distance and age difference did not foster growing relationships. Recently, the family has come together to celebrate weddings, anniversaries and the like. Barb says, "The best part for me is getting to know my cousins as adults and discovering what wonderful people they have grown into." Barb's design features elegant papers and embellishments that enhance the pale pink dresses that the cousins wore in one wedding.

Barb Hogan, Cincinnati, Ohio

Supplies: Textured vellum (Paper Adventures); silver cardstock (SEI); metal-rimmed tags, paper flowers, metal phrase eyelet (Making Memories); metal buttons (Hobby Lobby); ribbons (Stampin' Up!); spiral clip (7 Gypsies); silver charm (Card Connection); white acrylic paint; pink and white cardstocks; silver brads; pencil

good ole' bad hair days

Barb's mother's side of the family posed for this portrait in 1975. Her grandparents, parents, aunts and uncles, siblings and cousins came together for Thanksgiving. She says, "I just think that this picture is a riot. It's 'total seventies' to me . . . clothes, glasses, hair and home décor." The plaid papers resembled a style trend of the day and she used sandpaper to give everything an aged look.

Barb Hogan, Cincinnati, Ohio

Supplies: Patterned papers (Chatterbox); metal label holder (Making Memories); key (Westrim); sandpaper; transparency

mom and the boys

A life with so many boys is a grand adventure. One day the Taylor boys—Shannon's husband, brothers-in-law and sons—gathered for a day of bailing hay. She says, "All the boys were at the same place at one time which is rare. Then my mother-in-law stopped by so it was even rarer to have them all there. So I had to snap the shot. She loves it!" Shannon designed the page around the rustic clothes and backdrop, using mostly muted tones but adding clear blue elements for a pop of distinction.

Shannon Taylor, Bristol, Tennessee

Supplies: Patterned papers (C-Thru Ruler); transparency letters (Lay Over); twill ribbon (Li'l Davis Designs); letter buttons (Junkitz); rickrack (Hobby Lobby); letter stamps (Hero Arts); metal words (Go West Studios); black cardstock; black stamping ink; staples

sister-in-law

Roseanne is creating an album about each family member that includes special things about her relationship with each of them. While working on the one for her sister-in-law, she asked her to sit for a photo shoot. Roseanne captured her loveliness and personality in the photo. She says, "My sister-in-law is such a special person to me and has definitely become my best friend over the years. I have never really told her how I feel, so I made this page." This digital creation began with several downloaded elements. She used them to create the soft textures to coordinate with the botanical images.

Roseanne Miske, Monument, Colorado

Supplies: Image-editing software (Adobe Photoshop CS); Lilac Page Pak (CottageArts.net)

blessed be

High school graduation is a huge milestone! Margaret took advantage of her neice's graduation party to snap some multi-generational photos with the kids' great-grandmother, Dorothy. Margaret says, "I wanted to add the names of all the kids in the picture but instead of listing them in the journaling, I decided to add some flair by putting their names throughout to tie the whole layout together." Metal heart embellishments and gingham ribbon add a creative accent to the page.

Margaret Winters, Wichita, Kansas

Supplies: Patterned paper (Chatterbox); cardstock (Bazzill); mini brads, heart charm (Making Memories); ribbon (Offray); heart charm (Darice); transparency

4 generations

What a treasure to gather four generations in one family and to capture the event in a scrapbook page. Carrie seized the opportunity while visiting her grandmother in the summer of 2004. She imagined the "perfect" photo but decided that just having a photo was what really mattered. "Since we never know when life is going to deal a bad card, it's better to just take the pictures of it as it's happening and not worry about capturing perfection." With many patterns contained in the photo, Carrie diminished the distractions by printing in black-and-white.

Carrie Civinskas, Roscommon, Michigan

Supplies: Patterned papers, sticker tag, rub-on letters (SEI); ribbon (May Arts); letter and number stamps (PSX Design); black solvent ink (Tsukineko); blue, cream, cocoa and chocolate cardstocks and buttons (Bazzill); brown brads

tough guys

Family playtime knows no age limits. Wendy's son, 5, looks up to his cousin, 21. "My son has developed a wonderful relationship with him because David is a real crack-up! He's a kid himself and is still into all the fun things that my little guy thinks the world of—big muscles, video games and boxing (especially Rocky movies!)." This day, Wendy caught one manly moment and created a page about it. She kept the design masculine by using duct tape patterned paper, smudged tags and a small color palette.

Wendy Malichio, Bethel, Connecticut

Supplies: Patterned papers (Pebbles, Provo Craft); letter stickers (Pebbles); metal-rimmed tags, metal letter charm, washer word, ball chains, metal letter charm (Making Memories); label maker (Dymo); extreme eyelets (Creative Imaginations); black mini brads (American Tag Co.); dog tag (Chronicle Books); black eyelets; red brads; black stamping ink

4 cousins

"It's always a great photo op when four kids are together," says Dee. She loved these silly photos, taken on Christmas Eve, but said they presented a challenge. She decided that designing a traditional Christmas layout was not an option. She chose, instead, to accentuate the personalities of the four by using fun and funky patterned papers and tags along with plenty of embellishments.

Dee Gallimore-Perry, Griswold, Connecticut

Supplies: Patterned papers, tags (Basic Grey); monogram die cut (My Mind's Eye); letter stamps (Turtle Press); rub-on words, letters (Creative Imaginations, Making Memories); safety pins, blossoms, cardstock tags (Making Memories); definition sticker (Foofala); ribbons (Close To My Heart, May Arts); words twist tie (Pebbles); black stamping ink; mini brads; button; jump ring

brendan & lauren

Brendan, Dee's son, is six months older than his cousin, Lauren. They live just 25 minutes apart and often spend time together. Lauren loves to show her affection for him. Dee says, "Whenever she sees him, she just hugs him and mugs him up." Dee used warm brown tones for the majority of the page but used spots of blue to represent Brendan and pink for Lauren.

Dee Gallimore-Perry, Griswold, Connecticut

Supplies: Patterned papers, die cuts (KI Memories); letter stamps (Turtle Press); ribbon (Close To My Heart); definition (Boutique Trims); mini cardstock tag; white label holder, jump ring and pin (Making Memories); black stamping ink; pink brad; sandpaper

cousins

Danielle recently found this photo of herself and her cousin on their way to a wedding. They have a rare relationship. She says, "We are actually double-first cousins because our mothers are sisters and our fathers are brothers! . . . We had the same last name growing up and the same sets of grandparents. So we are all especially close," she says. Her journaling recounts how much fun the two had together and how she appreciates that their children can grow up together as well. For an eclectic look, Danielle combined a variety of retro papers and elements.

Danielle Thompson, Tucker, Georgia
Photo: Dolores Jenkins, Germantown, Tennessee

Supplies: Patterned papers (Colorbök, KI Memories, Li'l Davis Designs, Me & My Big Ideas, SEI); chipboard letters (Li'l Davis Designs); ribbon (Michaels); corner rounder scissors; yellow and purple cardstocks; staples; black pen

Our visit back to Illinois gave you a chance to visit with your "Great" Aunt Karen. This was such a special time for me to see you with her. Karen is the nicest most genuine woman. Every time we are together I am reminded of my Mother. They both have such similar loving personalities. Karen holds a special place in her heart for you. Never forget Addy how important Family is.....

hugs & kisses 04

best buds

best buds

Julie lost her mother 17 years ago and says, "Her sister (my Aunty K) shared with us her heart and love while we grew up. When I visit with Aunty K, I immediately feel a close bond to my mother." Now that Julie has her own family, she wants her daughter to know that special relationship. For this page, Julie chose soft colors to coordinate with the photos and to add feelings of love and peace.

Julie Geiger, Gold Canyon, Arizona

Supplies: Patterned papers, rub-on words (SEI); buttons (Doodlebug Design, Jesse James); ribbon (Offray); D rings (Prym-Dritz); powder blue, tan, pink and white cardstocks

only an aunt . . .

Mother's Day is often a time to get together with family. This year, Suzy's daughter, Sierra, and her Aunt Myrna posed in the back yard for some family pictures. Both of them glow in the sunshine as they share the warmth of family love. Suzy created this page to feature the beautiful photos and this perfect poem she found. Her dusty spring colors and minimal embellishments allow the photos to remain the focal point.

Suzy West, Fremont, California

Supplies: Patterned papers (SEI); ribbon (Michaels); pink, sage and cocoa cardstocks; photo corners; silk flowers; brown stamping ink

Only an Aunt...
can give hugs like a mother...
can keep secrets like a Sister...
and share love like a friend...

hands on

While Shannon went on a photo shoot with her mother, her boys came along. Thankfully, so did Uncle Andy to entertain them while she was at work. "My brother just has a way with them, so he kept them busy. He loves to get 'rough' with them. They jump on him and attack him," Shannon says. To complete the page, she connected the photos and journaling blocks with jump rings, adhering them to the page with foam adhesive for a "floating" look. Ribbons add soft texture to the page.

Shannon Taylor, Bristol, Tennessee

Supplies: Patterned paper, twill, jump rings, rub-on letters (Junkitz); ribbons (Rusty Pickle); rust and black cardstocks; foam adhesive

HANDS ON

Whenever the boys get together with Uncle Andy they have a blast. He loves to wrestle & flip them just as much as they love it. Uncle Andy Dandy Sugar Candy knows how to have a good time. We just wish he wasn't so busy! -2004

HAT TRICKS with Uncle Bill

You don't get a lot of chances to spend time with your Uncle Bill, but to see you interact with him, you'd never know it! You were 19 months old when these pictures were taken, but despite the fact that it had been awhile since you had seen each other, you certainly weren't shy. I'm not sure if that is a testament to your good memory, or just to the fact that Bill's such a fun uncle! On this particular day, we met Bill at a timeshare in Desoto, MO. You walked in and promptly swiped his hat. What's a little thievery between friends? August 2003

hat tricks

Susan's family enjoys a week together at a time share each summer. Upon arrival in Desoto, Missouri, Connor went straight to his Uncle Bill. "Connor and my brother usually don't get to see each other more than once or twice a year, so I was impressed that Connor went right to him," she says. "They immediately sat down and started playing with Bill's hat." The lighthearted design drew inspiration from the straw hat. Susan used matching colors, cut slits in two page edges and sewed paper yarn to the same sides.

Susan Cyrus, Broken Arrow, Oklahoma

Supplies: Raffia (DMD); metal-rimmed tag (Making Memories); black solvent ink (Tsukineko); brown and cream cardstocks; chalk

things i love about poppy

Once in a while, a relationship between grandfather and grandson carries the weight of a deep friendship. That is the case with Dee's father and her son. They are buddies who share many of the same interests. On Brendan's monthly sleepover at Mimi and Poppy's house, he and Grandpa can be found doing woodwork, science experiments, watching movies or the History Channel. Dee says, "My mom is always laughing about how those two get along when they're together. You'd think they'd been best friends for a hundred years." Dee's page elements coordinate with the photo's colors and textures.

Dee Gallimore-Perry, Griswold, Connecticut

Supplies: Patterned papers (Daisy D's, Li'l Davis Designs, Making Memories); letter stamps (Turtle Press); label maker (Dymo); triangular jump rings, safety pin (Making Memories); jewelry tag (Avery); date stamp (Office Max); love charm (Westrim); gingham ribbon; binder clip; black stamping ink

remembering grandfather

Each year, Tracy creates an album for her mom and dad of special memories and gives it to them for Christmas. Since her maternal grandfather had just passed away, it was difficult to create this one, but, she says, "I thought it was important to celebrate and memorialize my grandfather and all he gave to our family." She gathered photos from the years to create this layout. "When my mom got the album and got to that page, she cried and said it was absolutely perfect." Tracy included a tribute letter to him on the title page.

Tracy Weinzapfel Burgos, Ramona, California

Supplies: Patterned papers (Provo Craft); definitions (Making Memories); tan, avocado and cream cardstocks (Bazzill); mini brads; brown stamping ink; transparency

my girls

Jenn's photo of her bridal shower luncheon shows the love of the important women in her life: her sister, mother and grandmother. "We were going around taking candid shots and I was trying to get pictures of me with everyone. When I got this photo back from the developer, I knew I would treasure it forever." While trying to tie in all the clothing, Jenn chose various patterned papers. She sewed them to the background for a cohesive look and to honor her seamstress grandmother. To coordinate everything, she embellished using a variety of flowers on the left-hand side.

Jenn Brookover, San Antonio, Texas

Supplies: Patterned papers (American Crafts, Daisy D's, Making Memories, Paper Fever, PSX Design); rub-on letters (Chatterbox); wooden flowers, chipboard letter, chipboard phrase (Li'l Davis Designs); white grosgrain ribbon (Offray); mailbox letters, leather, paper flowers (Making Memories); word stickers (Chatterbox, Pebbles); vintage photo stamping ink (Ranger); buttons; brads; white rickrack; staples; transparency

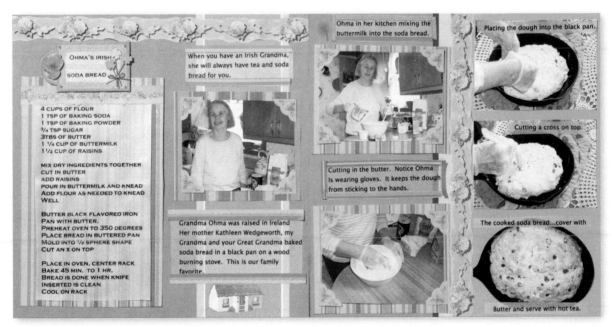

ohma's irish soda bread

Cathy began a family-recipes scrapbook and included tributes and history. She says, "My mom was born in the United States to Irish parents, she moved to Ireland, grew up there and returned to the United States when she was 18 . . . She learned to make Irish soda bread at home in her mother's kitchen. She used the 'black pans,' which is one of the secrets to a perfect soda bread." Cathy took these photos as her mother made the bread for a fund raiser. Her page design began with elements that reminded her of Ireland.

Cathy Leffler, Racine, Wisconsin

Supplies: Patterned papers (K & Company, Making Memories); embossed die cuts (K & Company); shamrock embellishment, house sticker (EK Success); avocado, pink and turquoise cardstocks; seed beads; silver vellum

grandma's love . . . golden

Living five hours away from her mom makes it difficult for Christine's family to visit often. When they do get together, Christine takes photos of her sons being themselves and sharing their love with Grandma. "I love watching my mom with the boys because I feel like I'm sneaking a glimpse into what it might've been like growing up as a kid—seeing what my childhood was like in third person," she says. Her design features rich colored papers and embellishments with black-and-white photos. Gold letters, glitter, charms and other elements enhance the title theme.

Christine Brown, Hanover, Minnesota

Supplies: Patterned paper (Carolee's Creations); mulberry papers (Pulsar Paper Products); fabric flowers (Jo-Ann Stores); gold frame corners (Michaels); flower punch (Family Treasures); sun, daisy, medium leaf punches (Marvy); small leaf punch (EK Success); buttons (Making Memories); gold twine (On The Surface); natural embroidery floss (DMC); gold embossing powder; raspberry stamping ink; raspberry, gold, white and cream cardstocks; key, heart charms (source unknown); metal craft sheet; gold eyelets; chalk; black pen

grandpa and mikey

Michelle keeps a camera with her at all times to capture simple but important moments like this one. "A photograph forever stops time, captures it right there in your hand!" she says "Childhood is so short in comparison to your lifetime. I don't want my children to forget a single moment, and I want our future generations to be able to look though their family history and to know the love that was there." Michelle kept her design simple, focusing the attention on the photo and creating a "picket fence" to lead the eye toward the photo.

Michelle Spiers, Kittrell, North Carolina

Supplies: Mini tags, letter stamps (Stampin'Up!); metal frame (Making Memories); beige, dark fawn, aloe vera cardstocks, vellum (Bazzill); pewter eyelets; chalk; sage stamping ink

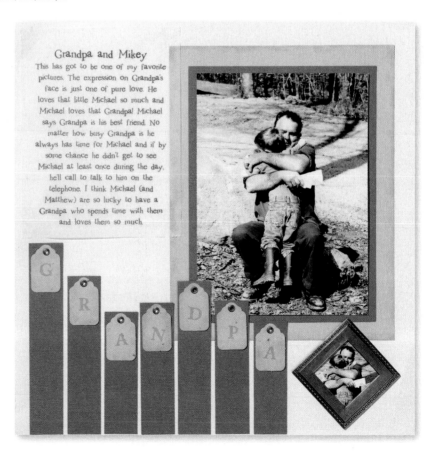

brendan and poppy

Dee occasionally browses through old photos, choosing some to use in her pages. "I find my perspective on the photo has really changed from when the picture was originally taken." This photo of her father holding her one-day-old son represents a classic example. She says that if she created the page years ago, she would have journaled about her son's beginning of life. Instead, she wrote about their strong, vital relationship now. To capture the feeling of new life and time, she used graphic ledger and definitions papers, along with the soft blues.

Dee Gallimore-Perry, Griswold, Connecticut

Supplies: Patterned papers (7 Gypsies, Creative Imaginations, Making Memories); letter stamps (Ma Vinci's Reliquary, Turtle Press); rub-on letters, metal photo corners (Making Memories); ribbon (Impress Rubber Stamps); woven label (Me & My Big Ideas); white and black snaps (Chatterbox); mini tag (Avery); date stamp; cream paint; chalk; paper clip; black stamping ink; label holder; black twill

grandma, my fondest memories

Losing a loved one can prompt us to record memories of his or her life. On the first anniversary of the death of her grandmother, Christine began writing down stories that she cherished. She put them together with photos and clip art to create this tribute page. Christine says, "When I was a kid, Grandma *was* Thanksgiving—everything always revolved around Grandma's house, and it was a time when the whole extended family got together." Her page gives a warm "grandma's attic" feeling, anchored by heartfelt stories of remembrance.

Christine Brown, Hanover, Minnesota

Supplies: Patterned papers (Anchor); flower cut-outs (Wallies); metal-rimmed tags, letter charms, metal word plaque, buttons (Making Memories); mini gold frames (Card Connection); gold label holder (www.twopea-sinabucket.com); mica (USArtQuest); skeleton leaves (Graphic Products Corp.); gold filigree charms (source unknown); black eyelets; embroidery floss; scrap fabric; black pen; twine; vellum

visible signs

Maria's father comes to visit from Venezuela every year, arriving on January 1 and staying for a week. As Maria looked at the photos from this impromptu photo session, she saw the striking similarities among family members. "Not exactly the same," she says, "but some features are very distinctive (the eyes are the same color, the red lips). I know that my dad loves to see himself reflected in his grandchildren, so I did the page to honor that." To keep the photos and the lighthearted journaling the focus, Maria used a bright background with simple embellishments.

Maria Gallardo-Williams, Cary, North Carolina

Supplies: Patterned papers (Karen Foster Design, Miss Elizabeth, Provo Craft); letter cut-outs (Diane's Daughters); red rickrack (AC Moore); black stamping ink; black pen

Visible signs that tell that you just might be a GALLARDO

IF

1. You have dark brown eyes.
2. You have very red lips (yes, even the boys have the red lips).
3. You have a quick temper but also a sweet disposition.
4. You are as stubborn as a mule...maybe even worse.
5. You are proud to say that you are a Gallardo. Abuelo worries that the name will die with him, but we'll do our best to keep it alive. After all, is not like we can hide it!

Remigio, Maite, Victoria and Nicholas. Cary, North Carolina. January 1st, 2005

circle of life

At a Father's Day picnic in June of 2004, Deanne took this photo of her daughters and their great-grandfather. She then created a page highlighting their special and treasured relationship. "Just six months after the picture was taken," she says, "my grandfather passed away suddenly. I have very few pictures of my girls with 'Papa,' so I can't tell you how special the picture is." Coordinating with the colors in the photograph, Deanne used patterned papers, ribbons and torn vellum to soften the page.

Deanne Schermerhorn, Cohoes, New York

Supplies: Patterned papers (Chatterbox, Mustard Moon); postage stamp letter cut-outs (Mustard Moon); rub-on letters, leather flower (Making Memories); clock hand stickers (EK Success); ribbons (Michaels, Offray); mini brad; white, red, blue and powder blue cardstocks; brown stamping ink; silver brad; vellum

CIRCLE OF LIFE

CHERISH

Trips in time, sharing, learning, hands stretched in love and caring.

From the old to the new and back around, the lessons are time capsules of love. Circles of life and living.

~Sandi Kelly 2004

grandparents

Cori created a mini album with stiched floral background papers to mirror a family quilt. She says, "I chose to stitch my background papers together to add interest to a simple design and to strengthen the feel of family ties." She listed the names of each family member along with a unique family tradition of the children sitting in the same spot on the staircase for holiday photos. Flowers and brads add a decorative touch.

Cori Dahmen, Vancouver, Washington

Supplies: Patterned papers (Provo Craft); eyelets, flower (Making Memories); leaves, flower sticker (EK Success); ribbon (May Arts); brads; vellum; ink

family gatherings

CHAPTER FIVE

You've got to love flashbacks of yester-year . . . the good old days growing up when there was less stress and more fun. Grown-up life is cluttered with day-to-day tasks and responsibilities, but amidst the mayhem we always find time to be with those most precious to us—even if it means crossing the miles to be present at an annual family re-union or cousin's wedding. It is at these family gatherings where we can relax, enjoy each other's company, share ex-citing milestones and family news and reminisce about days gone by.

Fortunately, there is a variety of fam-ily occasions that warrant presence in scrapbook pages. Among them are life-cycle events such as birthdays, bar mitzvahs, graduations, weddings, anniversaries and over-the-hill par-ties. Not to mention holiday celebra-tions such as Thanksgiving, Christ-mas, Hanukkah, Easter, the 4th of July, Cinco de Mayo, New Year's Eve, etc. Of course, picnics, barbe-cues and reunions are annuals in many clans. If you're searching for a creative and clever way to gather kin for no reason at all, suggest a Mardi Gras masquerade, Hawaiian luau or Caribbean beach party. The possibilities are endless, and all will delight in the energy and enthusi-asm of these family moments that turn into precious family memories.

My grandfather turned 80 that summer, so we decided it would be the perfect time for the family to go back to the island of Vieques in Puerto Rico where he grew up. It is truly amazing that all of us, from all over the U.S., could get together and share in his legacy.

—Jessie Baldwin

> "**Life** becomes harder for us when we live for others, but it also **becomes richer and happier.**"
>
> —*Albert Schweitzer*

A REUNION

LIKE NO OTHER

ONE
SMALL CARIBBEAN ISLAND

FOUR
GENERATIONS OF OUR FAMILY

23
FAMILY MEMBERS

80
YEARS OF MEMORIES

IN 2003 WE JOINED MY GRANDFATHER, LUIS HERNANDEZ, AS HE RETURNED TO VIEQUES, PUERTO RICO, HIS NATIVE ISLAND, TO SHARE HIS HISTORY WITH US... TALES OF SPARKLING WATER, RIDING HORSES, AND MARLIN FISHING. SO MANY MEMORIES ALIVE ON THAT TINY ISLAND... SO LUCKY WE ARE.

mau family rib fest

Lynne's husband is one of five siblings, including four brothers. They gather whenever they can but one gathering has become an annual event dubbed "Rib Fest." Jim, one of the brothers, hosts it every year. "The guys rent huge grills and spend all day seasoning, marinating and 'whatever-else-one-does' to ribs. Each family brings a side dish or dessert," she says. "Jim supplies the ribs." Her layout, using brown tones in graphic designs, features several new members of the Mau family, showing how it is growing.

Lynne Rigazio Mau, Channahon, Illinois

Supplies: Patterned papers (SEI); tag stickers (Pebbles); fabric letters, metal-rimmed tag, pocket (Making Memories); ribbons (May Arts); letter stickers (Sticker Studio); rub-on letters (Autumn Leaves); sage, brown and taupe cardstocks; twine; corner rounder; button; brown stamping ink; black pen; sandpaper

warning

Jean created this page about a family dream that began years ago. Her husband always wanted a Michigan lake house. He found land and, after moving to Michigan, their dream came true. She says, "A contractor completed the majority of the building, but all of us, including the children, did the painting. Now we are able to wake up to a pretty sunrise, fish at all hours of the day as well as enjoy boating and tubing." Her design inspiration came from a magazine advertisement for Kentucky tourism. She adapted it, using her own images and text.

Jean Marmo, Rockford, Michigan

Supplies: Peach and cream cardstocks (Bazzill); chalk pastels (Royal Talens); image-editing software (Microsoft Picture It!); craft wire

family

Life sometimes deals us challenges that can strain family relationships. This was the case for Colleen and some of her siblings. To alleviate some stress, her parents planned a family picnic. The day, filled with the laughter and silliness of children, helped mend relationships. Colleen created this page to tell the story of the event, showing the realities of family and to share with others her feelings about the importance of it. As she designed her page, she says "I wanted happy, playful papers to reflect what that day was for our family."

Colleen Stearns, Natrona Heights, Pennsylvania

Supplies: Patterned papers, stencil letter (Chatterbox); square brads (Happy Hammer); mailbox letters, printed twill (Making Memories); ribbon (May Arts); blue, taupe, rust and cocoa cardstocks (Bazzill); staples; transparency; black stamping ink

herrin family reunion

"There is only a tree left where the original old house stood, which belonged to my husband's great-grandparents. They had 12 children, who all had at least four children, who then had at least two each! Imagine the crowd!" Julie's family reunion, established over 30 years ago, boasts nearly 300 guests each year in Call, Texas. Her page features warm candid shots of family members surrounded by rich patterned papers. She created a pocket on the lower right corner to hold more photos.

Julie Johnson, Seabrook, Texas

Supplies: Patterned papers (Daisy D's); letter cut-outs (Foofala); rub-on words (C-Thru Ruler, Junkitz); sticker (Pebbles); paper flower, decorative brad, lace trim (Making Memories); corner rounder (Creative Memories); sandpaper; brown stamping ink

corbett

Holly's family tries to gather together yearly for a reunion. This particular year, the family celebrated at the "finally completed" retirement home of Grandma and Papa. On her monochromatic design, she included the names of all Papa's siblings, even though some were unable to attend. Holly's journaling captures the feelings of this special family time when she says, "New memories have been created, more stories have been told and tears have been shed for our lost ones. We leave with a bigger heart and a renewed sense of fondness for each other."

Holly Corbett, Central, South Carolina

Supplies: Patterned papers (Anna Griffin); monogram (My Mind's Eye); silk flowers (Wal-Mart); ribbons, white hinges (Making Memories, Offray); buttons (Little Black Dress Designs); square punch (EK Success); orange, peach, butterscotch and cream cardstocks; transparency; white acrylic paint; orange stamping ink

blodgett family reunion

Deborah's family has been holding reunions since 1932. This year, however, brought special meaning as she lost her father the year before. Deborah created an introspective page through meaningful journaling and definitions, embellished with symbolic elements. "I used the key along with the 'memories' definition to symbolize that our family memories are the keys to our past and future," she says.

Deborah Conken, Riverside, California

Supplies: Patterned papers (American Crafts, KI Memories); chipboard letter (Li'l Davis Designs); definitions (Hot Off The Press, Making Memories); copper-rimmed tag (DMD); petite frames (KI Memories); slide mount (Jest Charming); fibers; vellum; black stamping ink

family reunion

Having a family reunion for the first time certainly gives opportunities to take photos. Lynne's father's family got together for their first official reunion in August of 2004. Family members came from many parts of the country. Lynne's photos presented some small challenges as she felt they were not the best. "I really wanted to document the event since it was a first. So I grouped the shots together on the page and left a pocket for the journaling," she says.

Lynne Rigazio Mau, Channahon, Illinois

Supplies: Patterned papers (KI Memories); foam letter stamps, magnetic date stamp, label holder, ribbons (Making Memories); red and white cardstocks; black acrylic paint; gold and black pens; staples

stir fry

Heat a wok, add oil, fry some meat, toss in vegetables and voilá, dinner. Courtney says stir fry "is one of those healthy meals that my kids will actually eat, and I seriously love it. So, being such a big part of our lives, I wanted to be sure to document it." Usually her husband cooks, but for this page, Courtney gave her best effort to feed the family, with just a few moments of assistance. To design her page, she began with the enlarged photo of the wok. She added colorful patterned papers and handcut title letters.

Courtney Walsh, Winnebago, Illinois

Supplies: Patterned papers, word tag, white rivet (Chatterbox); circle punch (Emagination Crafts); ribbons (May Arts, Offray); letter stickers (Creative Imaginations); corner rounder; red, black, blue and tan cardstocks; staple; black stamping ink; sandpaper; black pen

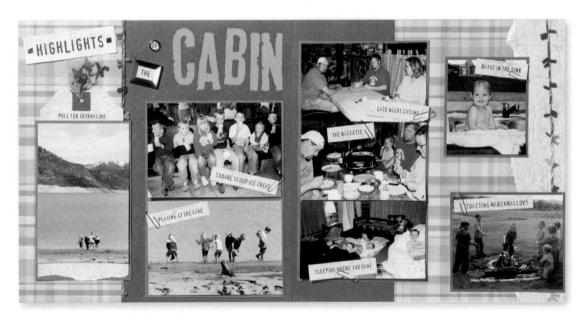

highlights of the cabin

Every Memorial Day for years, Shaunte's and her neighbors' families go to a cabin. Having children nearly the same age, everyone has a playmate, keeping them out of trouble. The weekend "is purely for relaxing," she says. "I wanted to capture the simple moments—playing cards at night, the kids all sleeping in the same room in sleeping bags, giggling all night long, a lot of just plain doing nothing!" Shaunte's spread, featuring rustic, earthy colors, combined several photos onto single mats and kept embellishments simple for a clean and engaging look.

Shaunte Wadley, Lehi, Utah

Supplies: Patterned papers (Chatterbox, Karen Foster Design); concho, mini frame (Scrapworks); foam letter stamps, square brads (Making Memories); fibers (Fibers By The Yard); square punch (Punch Bunch); square hole punch (Fiskars); sage and rust cardstocks; sage acrylic paint; paper clips

picnic at the park

As a child, Rachael and her brothers spent a week with their grandmother every summer, finding plenty of time to go to Hood Park, just around the corner. Recently, when one brother came to New Hampshire, they revisited the park. "It was a rare treat to go back to such a special place from our childhood and share that experience with our children . . . I don't think they quite understood the sentimental feelings that Jamie and I shared, being back at the park that held so many fond memories."

Rachael Giallongo, Auburn, New Hampshire

Supplies: Patterned paper, foam letter stamps (Making Memories); acrylic charms (Doodlebug Design); label maker (Dymo); evergreen cardstock (Bazzill); copper brads; twine; buttercream acrylic paint; black pen

family together

Deanna took these photos in 1999 and later realized how special they were. It was the last time her family celebrated all together at "Mamaw's" house. Her journaling tells the story of the weekend and reflects on the last part of Mamaw's life: "It's great to have a memory of a time when things were just as they should be." To create the page, Deanna used a scrapbooking kit. When she saw the photos of her niece in the orange shirt and bicycle helmet, she says, "the paper popped into my head and the layout flowed from there."

Deanna Koontz, Petersburg, Indiana

Supplies: Patterned papers, acrylic charms (KI Memories); foam letter stamps (Making Memories); flower die cuts (Sizzix); fibers (Fibers By The Yard); square punch (Creative Memories); lime, white and orange cardstocks (Bazzill); acrylic paint; white gel pen

making perogies

This annual event began before Rachael's husband was born and continues today as the family gathers on Christmas Eve. "Slowly but surely, this generation is teaching the next generation the recipe and fine art of rolling out the perfect perogie. We usually spend about five hours together in the process," she says. "The page I created was very special to me because my husband added his family recipe in his own handwriting." Rachael added this page to a scrapbook of family recipes and history to inspire her children to continue important traditions.

Rachael Giallongo, Auburn, New Hampshire

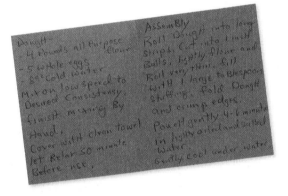

Supplies: Patterned papers, vellum, phrase stickers (K & Company); letter stickers (Creative Imaginations, EK Success); metal letters, rub-on words (Making Memories); ribbon (Stampin' Up!); buttons (Junkitz); letter cut-outs, library pocket (Designer's Library); label maker (Dymo); gold photo corners (Canson); mini brads (Chatterbox); black embroidery floss; sage cardstock; black pen

a family tradition

Sometimes family traditions come from loss. Karen says, "My father-in-law grew up with 10 kids in his family in a small town in Arkansas. In 1980, his mother passed away and the children decided to get together every year to keep in touch and remember their mother." Each year 50-75 attend to play volleyball, eat, socialize and entertain. "Guitars, both electric and acoustic, fiddles and a harmonica make the best homemade music around," she says. To incorporate a variety of photos, along with journaling and a title, Karen used a page template to help arrange everything.

Karen Rhea, Saint Peters, Missouri

Supplies: Letter stickers (Pebbles); epoxy word sticker (Creative Imaginations); heart punch (Marvy); music note die cuts (Accu-Cut); definition (Foofala); page template (Deluxe Designs); taupe, cream, butter, avocado, red and black cardstocks

our october tradition

Ursula recounts that "not long before I made this pumpkin page, I was reading an article in a magazine about how important family traditions are and that it . . . bonds the family together. It hit me that our trip to the pumpkin patch was something we did every year, and it had turned into our annual tradition." She used rich tones from the photos to unite her page, and she included homey touches with handmade paper and stitching.

Ursula Page, Thomasville, Georgia

Supplies: Green handmade paper, metal charm (www.scrapsahoy.com); metal letters, square brads (Making Memories); bleach pen (Clorox); mesh paper (Magenta); rivets (Chatterbox); shipping tag (www.twopeasinabucket.com); mini frame (Foofala); pumpkin cut-out (EK Success); orange embroidery floss (DMC); rust and cream cardstocks; chalk; black pen

stringfellow competition

It was a dark and stormy night, but Susan's family made the best of it when the power went out. Her husband, Perry, taught the boys how to play poker while Susan chuckled and took photos. She shot close-ups to show the personalities in their poker faces. "Alex could bluff like a pro right off. Chris was about average, he is always calm and in control, but . . . poor Brett couldn't bluff to save his life. He lets his emotions and thoughts show all over his face." She created her title by decoupaging tissue paper letters on the spread.

Susan Stringfellow, Cypress, Texas

Supplies: Patterned paper (Remember When); tissue paper letters (7 Gypsies); decoupage paste (Plaid); library pocket, tag, walnut ink (Altered Pages); card stamp (source unknown); rub-on words, ribbon buckle (Making Memories); faux playing card stickers (EK Success); ribbons, fibers (Fibers By The Yard, Michaels); cork embellishments (LazerLetterz); brown cardstock; transparency; shirt clips; black brads; black and brown stamping inks

art of pingpong

Sande's family has enjoyed a pingpong dynasty, of sorts. She says, "I grew up playing pingpong on a homemade pingpong table. My dad grew up playing ping pong so he made us a table." Since it is an activity that she, her husband and their boys agree on, it is one they pursue at home or when traveling. To create the dramatic color effect, Sande used image-editing software to layer the photo with black-and-white, while masking the paddles to keep them colored.

Sande Krieger, Salt Lake City, Utah

Supplies: Patterned papers, twill and large letter cut-outs (Scenic Route Paper Co.); letters (Foofala); letter stickers, paper clip (EK Success); wooden letter (Provo Craft); image-editing software (Adobe Creative Suite); label maker (Dymo); word stickers (Making Memories); coated linen thread (Scrapworks); library pocket (Bazzill); tag (Office Max); acrylic paint; twine; mini brads; sandpaper; black pen

trivia time

On any given day, children do lots of normal, yet memorable, things. This was the case at Annette's house when, she says, "Nothing exciting was happening, and we just wanted a little bit of family time. So we pulled out the trusty board game and had a little fun." Her journaling recounts that playing games often fills their family time. To design her page, she began with a cardstock base and added splashes of patterned papers to coordinate with the photo.

Annette Pixley, Scappoose, Oregon

Supplies: Patterned papers, die cuts, sticker (KI Memories); rub-on letters (Scrapworks); rub-on word (Doodlebug Design); date stamp (Making Memories); chalk inks (Clearsnap); colored brads (Happy Hammer); white, black, tan and green cardstocks

the need for speed

After waiting in line, Sande and her two sons climbed aboard a Viking boat ride, facing each other at the center. She sat wedged against her younger son and actually moved to get the shot. "It's a technique called panning," she says. "You set your shutter speed at approximately 1/30th of a second . . . Depress the shutter but continue moving." This technique gives the background a blur and the subject a sharp focus. Her journaling tells how she and her son share this deep sense of adventure.

Sande Krieger, Salt Lake City, Utah

Supplies: Patterned papers (7 Gypsies, Li'l Davis Designs, Memories in the Making, Scenic Route Paper Co.); words transparency (7 Gypsies); image-editing software (Adobe Creative Suite); beveled nailheads (American Tag Co.); courage charm (source unknown); paper clip (EK Success); decorative brad, label holder (Making Memories); mini tags (Office Max); transparency; silver and cream brads; leather cording; black pen; cork

the pavilion

Many people have memories of family traditions from their youth and now, with families of their own, continue them. Nancy's favorites from childhood include visiting Myrtle Beach. She and her siblings have had two reunions there. "We do the same things we did when we were young, including going to the Pavilion to eat snow cones and ride the rides," she says. "I wanted my layout to reflect the nostalgia of my childhood as well as the fun we had the day we were there." Nancy accomplished this by using retro colors, a funky font and scattered buttons.

Nancy McCoy, Gulfport, Mississippi

Supplies: Patterned papers (Basic Grey); square punch (Marvy); blue and rust cardstocks (Bazzill); twine; buttons; gold eyelets; mini brads

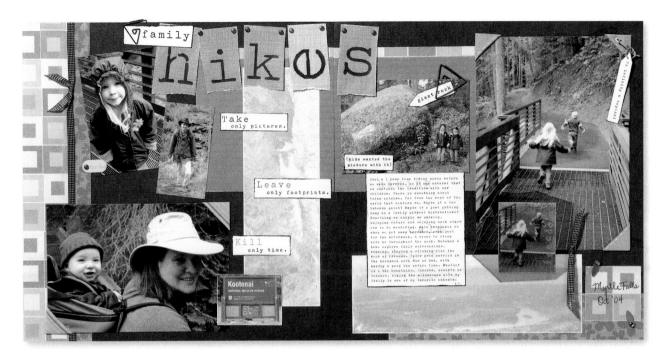

family hikes

Sheila's family departed from their home on an overcast day to hike to a waterfall. When they arrived, it began to rain but the family still wanted to go. They dressed in warm clothes and set out. "The kids ran ahead on the trail. I can still see them in my mind; the older two had their arms out to the side, pretending to fly," she says. Her spread included a range of images from the day, complemented by the fall-colored papers and embellishments.

Sheila Doherty, Coeur d'Alene, Idaho

Supplies: Patterned papers (Chatterbox); triangular paper clips (Scrapbook Sensation); ribbon (Michaels); mini plastic word tag (Eyelet Outlet); fabric photo corners, safety pin, photo turns (Making Memories); mica (USArt Quest); letter stamps (PSX Design); watermark stamping ink (Tsukineko); distress ink; embossing powder; navy cardstock; brads; twine; black stamping ink; black pen; sandpaper

child of my child

Sometimes a photo dramatically sets the tone for a page. "The minute I took it, I knew it was something special," says Becky, of this photo. "Sam and my dad have an amazing relationship. He truly is her favorite playmate." Becky captured the essence of this with a poem she found on the Internet. A few delicate embellishments such as decorative brads, ribbon and rub-ons complete the look and help tell the story.

Becky Pogatchnik, Proctor, Minnesota

Supplies: Rub-on letters, decorative brads (Making Memories); ribbons (Michaels); distress ink (Ranger); sage and white cardstocks (Bazzill)

camping with riley

"I'm not sure what made me think camping with a 3-year-old would be a good idea," says Holly in the opening sentence of her journaling. She and her husband ventured just 40 minutes from home to camp, roast marshmallows, hike, canoe and even play miniature golf at their campsite. She was inspired by a layout found online and says, "I liked the multiple small pictures used to tell a story." Holly embellished the page with rustic elements, including using fibers resembling rope to spell out her title.

Holly Pittroff, Huntersville, North Carolina

Supplies: Patterned paper (Cloud 9 Design, Karen Foster Design); tree bark tag (Wübie); patterned vellum (Paper Company); fibers (Great Balls of Fiber, Xpressions); letter stickers (Pebbles); brown embroidery floss; brown cardstock; black pen; burlap; bamboo; eyelet; chalk

finding nemo & friends

When Jessie' family visited the Scripps Aquarium in San Diego, her children looked in every tank for Nemo and his friends. Near the end of the day they came to the tropical tank. Jessie first shot with a flash but it washed out the images. "When I took the photo without the flash, I took a deep breath and rested my elbows on the ledge to keep the camera steady," she says, giving her this surprising image. She used colors to complement the blue cast on her family's faces and to coordinate with the striking fish.

Jessie Baldwin, Las Vegas, Nevada

Supplies: Patterned paper (Sandylion); embossed paper (Jennifer Collection); rub-on letters, silver brads (Making Memories); metal fish (source unknown); red and yellow cardstocks

gone crabbin

After Molly's boys returned from their "crabbin" trip with Daddy, they couldn't wait to get the photos back and talked about the event for days. When the photos did come, Molly says that her husband opened them with the boys and their faces lit up. He told her, "This is like one of those MasterCard commercials, you know, 'Priceless.'" The inspiration for the page came from that statement. Molly's rustic design includes inking, giving an earthy feel, and mesh ribbon, reminiscent of crab nets.

Molly Freed, Orange, Texas

Supplies: Patterned vellum (Chatterbox); pogs (Autumn Leaves); die-cut letters (QuickKutz); foam letter stamps (Making Memories); blue, taupe, celery and orange cardstocks; mesh; twine; orange acrylic paint; brown stamping ink

joys of being a child

While on a vacation to learn about American history, Sande and her family played "dollars for questions." Sande asked questions about history and presentations they had seen. When her boys answered correctly, they received Williamsburg dollars to spend in the park. She says, "They loved this game and would eagerly listen and participate in every activity so they would be ready for the questions." Her page features action photos taken of a favorite game, Nine Pins. She chose neutral colors along with striking red accents to coordinate with the photos.

Sande Krieger, Salt Lake City, Utah

Supplies: Patterned papers (K & Company, Sticker Studio); round label holders, wood letters, red safety pin (Li'l Davis Designs); natural printed twill, walnut ink (7 Gypsies); red printed twill, decorative brads, washer word (Making Memories); epoxy sticker (K & Company); brown stamping ink; brads; brown cardstock

happy birthday to us

Scrapbookers attend or host birthday parties over the course of a year but, "we usually only get one or two 'scrappable' photos," Bela says. "If I were to create a layout for every birthday, my goodness, that would be a lot of pages, so I decided to combine them all in one." Included in the layout are parties for her son, as he turned 1, along with celebrations for her husband, in-laws, mother and herself. Bogey, her dog, showed his party spirit too.

Bela Luis, Winnipeg, Manitoba, Canada

Supplies: Patterned paper (NRN Designs); letter stickers (Doodlebug Design); rub-on letters (Scrapworks); ribbons; white cardstock; birthday candle

easter

Danielle's family celebrated Cooper's first Easter at Collanwolde Fine Arts Center in Atlanta. "Callanwolde is a place where you can go to take art classes. . .listen to fine music and see their art gallery," she says. "They also do yearly events, such as this Easter egg hunt." With azaleas blooming and families scampering about to find eggs, it was a perfect spot for spring photos. Danielle's page is rich with spring images, embellishments and colors. She created texture by adding dimensional paint over a stencil and coloring it after it dried. Fabric elements add softness to the spread.

Danielle Thompson, Tucker, Georgia

Supplies: Patterned papers, large frame stencil (Anna Griffin); letter stamps (PSX Design, Stamp Craft); foam letter stamps, spiral clip (Making Memories); vintage Easter Bunny image (Dover Publications); velvet fabric (Jo-Ann Stores); laser-cut butterflies (Li'l Davis Designs); dimensional paint (Delta); flower stickers (La Petites); rhinestone pin (EK Success); fabric flowers (Prima); ink jet iron-on transfer (June Taylor); watermark ink (Tsukineko); black cardstock; stick pin; white buckle; black ribbon; frog closure; chalk; black and gold stamping ink; white, purple and black acrylic paints

we give thanks

Sometimes tragedy strikes but after the dust settles, there are reasons to be thankful. When Sheredian's son was paralyzed playing football, the family struggled to make sense of the accident while Andre struggled for life. Four months later he came home from the hospital. Four months after that, the extended family celebrated Thanksgiving together. "It has been a hard adjustment for the family, but none of us can imagine how much harder it is for Andre. Yet, he takes each day in stride and tries to maintain a positive attitude," she says. "We have much to be thankful for because we still have Andre."

Sheredian Vickers, The Woodlands, Texas

Supplies: Patterned paper (Creative Imaginations); metal letters, silver buckle (Making Memories); label maker (Dymo); rub-on word (SEI); ribbons (Making Memories, Michaels); letter stamps (Hero Arts); tag; black, white, cream and rose cardstocks; silver brads; chalk; corner rounder; black stamping ink

father's day

Carolyn's grandmother made scrapbooks and has albums from the late 1800s. Carolyn scans and prints images from the albums to create pages. This page showcases the family's 1946 Father's Day celebration. During that time of war, Carolyn's mother took many photos to send to her father in Germany. "There aren't that many photos of both my of grandfathers together, so I was excited to enlarge that piece of the photo," she says. "It was probably because one of them was always behind the camera." To accent her page, she used antique images, neutral colors and red accents.

Carolyn Cleveland, Maysville, Georgia

Supplies: Patterned papers, stickers (Deluxe Designs); red flower, gingham fabric (www.scrapaddict.com); stickers (Pebbles); decorative brads, leather frame (Making Memories); stamp stickers (K & Company); number stickers (Hot Off The Press); stamping inks; red and brown cardstocks; vintage postcard; chalk

believe in family

Celebrating a little one's first Christmas brings family members to meet the new addition. It is a great time to share the love of family. Danielle's son, Cooper, was just 3 months old, and she took photos of him with everyone. To design her page, she says, "I got the color palette and rich textures and patterns from the Indian, Asian flavor of the room. You can see an Indian tapestry in the background of the large photo." She added texture to the page by layering paper, mesh, photos, wallpaper cut-outs and embellishments.

Danielle Thompson, Tucker, Georgia

Supplies: Patterned papers (7 Gypsies, Paper Company); embossed papers (www.handmade.us, www.hollanders.com); mesh (Magic Mesh); metal plaques, rub-on word, hinge (Making Memories); gold leaf (Houston Art Inc.); woven labels (Me & My Big Ideas); heart stickers, slide mounts, clock vellum, letter stickers (EK Success); word charm (Pebbles); decorative corner punch (Anna Griffin); black stamping ink; red metallic thread; gold pen; sandpaper; pink cardstock; eyelets; flower cut-outs; transparency

xmas memories

While moving, Tracy's mother found a box in the back of her closet, which she gave to Tracy. It was full of snapshots of Tracy's childhood memories. Tracy began cropping them for "Book of Me" scrapbooks for her daughters. When creating, she says, "The story for each is the focus of the layout. I include photos that help tell the story and that are of the best quality from the box." For this Christmas layout, she shared many childhood memories in her journaling and used torn papers, photos and a bow to create a wreath shape.

Tracy Austin, Bossier City, Louisiana

Supplies: Patterned papers (Flair Designs, Me & My Big Ideas); foam letter stamps, magnetic date stamp (Making Memories); ribbons (K & Company, Offray); jewelry tags (American Tag Co.); green stamping ink; cream and green acrylic paints; transparency; staples

cherish

Joanna created a mini album to celebrate some of her family's traditions, including hiking in the Blue Ridge Mountains and visiting petting zoos. She says, "I wanted to combine both an 'old' and 'new' style to it." She used computer-generated borders to introduce each page but felt that handwritten journaling would be more appropriate to reflect an old-fashioned way of doing things. A wooden frame, definition sticker and transparency create a unique accent for the cover.

Joanna Bolick, Fletcher, North Carolina
Photos: Mark Bolick, Fletcher, North Carolina

Supplies: Album, definition stickers (Making Memories); patterned papers (Rusty Pickle); rub-on stitches (Autumn Leaves); wooden frame (Li'l Davis Designs); cardstocks; transparency

family homes

CHAPTER SIX

Many people envision a home as a place of tranquility, simple beauty and wholesome charm. It is the place where we recharge our spirits, entertain friends and express our identities through unique décor and furnishings. But as many families know, especially those with kids and pets, home can also be a place of mass hysteria! Cooking, cleaning, washing, ironing, repairing, mending and, oh yes, organizing can turn the idyllic image of the perfect family home topsy-turvy. But amidst the frenzy, a family home resonates the laughter, love, joy and happiness felt by its inhabitants. It serves as a personal sanctuary when we want to escape the grueling demands of the world, exhibits the warmth and affection of loved ones who share its

walls and echoes both the quiet and sometimes boisterous rhythm of daily life.

Scrapbook pages that feature your home can include places of living and leisure, cooking and eating spaces, children's rooms, gardens or any room that reveals your personal sense of style, whether it be country charm or urban chic. Snapshots that include loved ones and animal companions enhance your artwork by displaying the emotional connection to your physical surroundings. Whether you choose to show every unique angle or that one special jewel of a room, your page will shine as it gives observers a glimpse into the place you call home.

The kitchen is where the action is. Good food is conducive to great conversations. I suppose even as a child the kitchen was my favorite room in the house.

—*Samantha Walker*

OUR HOME

2005

First It sounded like a good idea... [we s]et out to buy paint to give our house a little [colo]r—of course I fell in love with the Venetian [plas]ter finish that Home Depot had on display--I [had] no idea that the technique would take three [gall]ons of plaster and 5 days to complete one room-- [not] to mention that I had another gallon of red [plas]ter waiting for the bathroom walls. In that same [trip] to Home Depot, we decided that the old trim [was] just...well...too old and too funky looking (it was [this] awful fake wood vinyl wrapped stuff that [dar]kened in any of our sunny windows) so we [bou]ght new trim and baseboard. The new trim [spaw]ned the idea that we would need crown [mol]ding to complete the look. Soon we were [pai]nting the doors to match the new trim. You [wou]ld think that that was enough change to make [our] house the homey place we had envisioned. [How]ever, the new paint clashed with the old carpet, [whi]ch actually, just about everything clashed with [tha]t purple hued carpet that the original homeowners [thou]ght was just grand—sure it may have gone well [wi]th there stuff, but it never really worked with our [thi]ngs. I suggested that we get new carpet [down]stairs to fix the dilemma. Jonathan wasn't too [ke]en on spending more money, but he agreed that [th]e old carpet just didn't work. Instead of carpeting [th]e living room, He suggested that we put laminate [flo]oring in the living room and rip up our kitchen [flo]or and continue the laminate in there. I wasn't [s]ure about laminate in the living room, but agreed to [i]t as long as I could find a nice area rug to give the [ro]om a little warmth. Soon we found ourselves laying [o]ur own laminate and purchasing carpet for the [f]amily room. Of course, while the carpet layer came [t]o measure, I told him to go ahead and measure for [t]he stairs since you could see them from the family [r]oom. Our walls looked beautiful and now they [m]atched the carpet and the new laminate, but we [n]eeded something more to complete the look—we [b]ought some framed prints and got some fun new [d]ishes to add a splash of color. Did I mention that [w]e got new window treatments as well, oh and [n]ew faucets in the bathrooms, and two new light [f]ixtures? It's been four months since we started our ["l]ittle" project and we are so close to being finished. [W]e just have a few more pieces of crown molding to [p]ut up and some nail holes to fill...or at least that is [w]hat we think. If I had known how much work this [p]roject was going to be in the beginning, I may have [sh]ied away from doing a remodel. However seeing [th]e end result, I realize that the entire process has [ce]rtainly been worth the effort. Our hard work turned our house into a home.

home hangouts

Jeniece highlighted the places in her home that family members enjoy. For her, it is a "dream come true" craft room. Her husband avoids a long commute on Fridays by using his home office. The kids love the finished basement filled with toys, foosball and the pool table. After completing the page, Jeniece says, "It will be interesting to see how their favorite places (as well as the rooms themselves) change over the years." Her design inspiration began with patterned paper featuring doors, reminding her of home. She embellished the page with a metal frame resembling bricks and various keys.

Jeniece Higgins, Lake Forest, Illinois

Supplies: Patterned papers (Anna Griffin, Basic Grey, Mustard Moon); letter stamps (FontWerks, Hero Arts, Ma Vinci's Reliquary, PSX Design); key charms (EK Success, Rusty Pickle); metal frame (Provo Craft); cream acrylic paint; white cardstock; transparency; ribbons; black stamping ink

Here are the Higgins Family's favorite places to hang out at home:
Above photo: The basement—this is where the kids can be found playing Play Station, pool, foosball or with toys.

Right photo: The hobby room—this is where mom hangs out late at night making scrapbook pages.

Bottom photo: The office—this is where Dad works on Fridays so he doesn't have to drive to the city.

By the summer of 2003 we'd moved nine times in 15 years. It was hard on all of us, especially the kids. Each place was just another rental house, not our own, not personal. After Bri's dad passed away we realized that the kids needed a place to call their own, a place to call home. A place where they could hang pictures and choose wall colors and feel like they belonged. So I got a new job, we moved north to Vancouver and we bought our first home.

for our kids

Because of jobs, Cori and her family moved nine times in 15 years. Then, Cori and her husband decided to settle in and stay put. They landed in Vancouver, Washington, and bought their first house. Cori shares her feeling about this by featuring her children in front of their house. Picking up the colors in the kids' clothing and on the house, she chose patterned papers. With a color-blocked background and stitching, the page gives the impression of a quilt.

Cori Dahmen, Vancouver, Washington

Supplies: Patterned papers (Chatterbox); rub-on letters, chipboard letters (Making Memories); buttons (Hillcreek Designs); twill (May Arts); blue and celery cardstocks; green paint

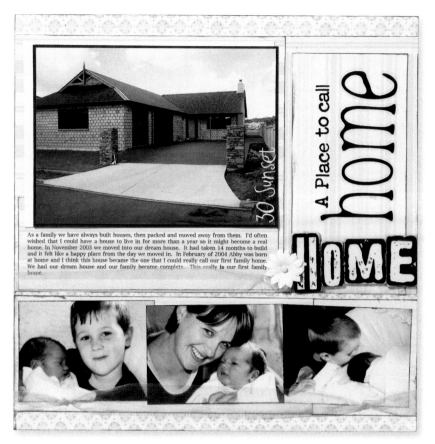

a place to call home

Being married to a builder, Nic has spent time moving from house to house. This page shows the one she first considered her home. "I had a home birth with Abby, and having our only daughter join us while we were living there was certainly significant," she says. Her page design grew out of that significant event. She used soft, feminine papers with black-and-white photos, revealing the strong emotions that she has for this home.

Nic Howard, Pukekone, South Aukland, New Zealand

Supplies: Patterned papers (Melissa Frances); rub-on letters, paper flower (Making Memories); letter stickers (Mustard Moon); chipboard letters (Li'l Davis Designs); chalk ink (Clearsnap); organza ribbon; white and black cardstocks; yellow brad; chestnut stamping ink

point. click. buy.

Susan's investing brought about some great rewards. "We bought some AOL stock during the tech boom and were amazed to watch it shoot up in price and then split . . . several times," she says. "Each time we met with the builders to talk about brick or paint or some other detail, they wanted . . . an update on how AOL stock was doing. By the time we were finished building, we were all referring to it as 'The house that AOL built.'" She included an AOL disk and packaging images to complete the page.

Susan Cyrus, Broken Arrow, Oklahoma

Supplies: Metal plaque, metal-rimmed tags (Making Memories); key sticker (EK Success); ball chain (Boxer Scrapbook Productions); CD and packaging (AOL); gray and green cardstocks

our new home

"I was inspired to do the layout because if you move around a lot in your life, you'd like to remember just where you've lived. I don't remember much about my childhood homes, so I wanted something for myself to remember and my children to recall in later years," says Debbie about her recently purchased house. She used photos from the realtor's brochure and one she took while on "walk-though" before they purchased the home. Using striped vellum, she created a frame to resemble shutters and the rest of the page flowed from there.

Debbie Coe, Suwanee, Georgia

Supplies: Patterned paper, patterned vellum, rivets (Chatterbox); transparency words (My Mind's Eye); letter stamps (All Night Media); key, die-cut keyhole (Li'l Davis Designs); home quote (DieCuts with a View); black stamping ink

the house where i grew up

Before making an "All About Me" book, Bela got some page ideas from a scrapbooking Web site. This page is one of her first in the album. She says, "I liked the idea of using the black-and-white photo because my mom has a black-and-white photo like this of me as a baby." Bela kept the page simple with hidden journaling featuring fond memories of her teenage life at this house. "I left this driveway the first time I ever drove a car, and then again in a limo the day I got married."

Bela Luis, Winnipeg, Manitoba, Canada

Supplies: Patterned paper (7 Gypsies); compass concho (source unknown); label holder (www.twopeasinabucket.com); tags (2DYE4); hinges; twine; black, brown, cocoa and cream cardstocks; eyelets

my home

After getting married and living in an apartment for a couple of years, Bela and her husband bought a loft. Her journaling takes the reader on a tour of the locations of the five homes she's lived in over 28 years. It also tells of their restlessness to find a home big enough for them, their dog and a new little one. At the time, they didn't find what they were looking for but she says, "We're hoping by the end of the summer to have a new home with a nice big backyard."

Bela Luis, Winnipeg, Manitoba, Canada
Photo: Joel Ross Photography, Winnipeg,
Manitoba, Canada

Supplies: Patterned paper (Treehouse Designs); embossed pewter sticker (Magenta); page pebble (Making Memories); brown cardstock (Bazzill); gingham ribbon; black pen

My home

I am a city girl at heart. I was born and raised in the beautiful city of Winnipeg, MB, Canada, and have lived here my whole life. In the past 28 years, I have lived in 5 different homes. First was at 548 Sherbrook. We lived with my family there from the time that I was born till the age of 2. When my parents had saved up to buy a house of their own, we moved to 327 Arlington. We stayed there until I was 15, and then my parents chose to move to a quieter neighbourhood, so off we went to 24 Macklin, a nice house in Garden City. When I got married, we decided to rent an apartment for a few years, so we lived in Evergreen Towers on Osborne Street. We loved it there, but soon felt that it was time to stop paying rent and start paying a mortgage. We've been at the Ashdown Warehouse for three years, and we love it. It will be hard to leave our loft condo next year, when we look for a house for our growing family. Winnipeg is a great place to live, the economy is good, the cost of living is great, the weather in the summer is gorgeous (but too cold in the winter) and there's always something to do. For now, this home is where my heart is.

09/13

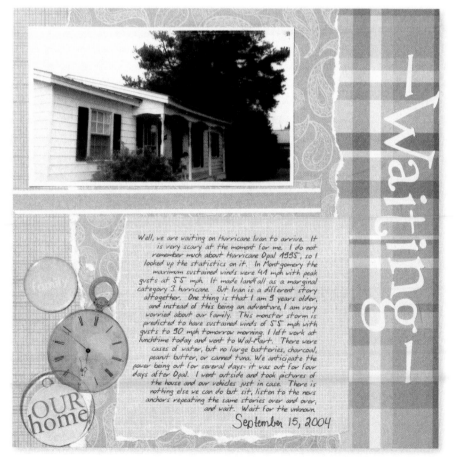

Well, we are waiting on Hurricane Ivan to arrive. It is very scary at the moment for me. I do not remember much about Hurricane Opal 1995, so I looked up the statistics on it. In Montgomery the maximum sustained winds were 41 mph with peak gusts at 55 mph. It made landfall as a marginal category 3 hurricane. But Ivan is a different story altogether. One thing is that I am 9 years older, and instead of this being an adventure, I am very worried about our family. This monster storm is predicted to have sustained winds of 55 mph with gusts to 90 mph tomorrow morning. I left work at lunchtime today and went to Wal-Mart. There were cases of water, but no large batteries, charcoal, peanut butter, or canned tuna. We anticipate the power being out for several days- it was out for four days after Opal. I went outside and took pictures of the house and our vehicles just in case. There is nothing else we can do but sit, listen to the news anchors repeating the same stories over and over, and wait. Wait for the unknown.
September 15, 2004

waiting

Southern living can bring a hurricane to your front door. While Amy's family waited for Hurricane Ivan to come ashore in 2004, she says, "I was feeling terribly anxious about the situation and decided to create the scrapbook page. I thought perhaps I could allay some of my fears by writing them down." She also wrapped her scrapbooks in bags to prevent possible damage. Since her husband had asked her to take photos for possible insurance information, she included one on her page. Although Ivan did come ashore with great force, her home and family remained safe.

Amy Brown, Eclectic, Alabama

Supplies: Patterned papers (Chatterbox); letter stickers (Creative Imaginations); epoxy stickers (Creative Imaginations, K & Company); rub-on words (SEI); black pen

a house is a home

It's difficult to express how fully a home can impact our lives. Andrea's page is the beginning of an entire album dedicated to her childhood home and the moments shared there. "I wanted to convey the sense of memories lying just inside the door of this home. I created the little book with a door handle on it with a photo of the front door. When you open the book, some additional memories and photos are found," she says. She limited the page's colors to blue and gray to offer a peaceful and grounded feeling.

Andrea Lyn Vetten-Marley, Aurora, Colorado

Supplies: Patterned papers (Diane's Daughters); copper handle (Foofala); stamps (Club Scrap, Hero Arts, Inkadinkado, Paper Inspirations, Prickley Pear Rubber Stamps, PSX Design, Stamp Craft); gray and black cardstocks (Bazzill); black stamping ink; keys; blue rickrack; sandpaper

home sweet home

After Dawn and her family moved into their new home, Dawn wanted to create a layout for her daughter's scrapbook. Kailee, like many 2-year-olds, was fairly unpredictable when being photographed. Dawn says, "I started saying to her, 'show me your big beautiful house' with lots of enthusiasm and putting my arms up in the air trying to make it fun for her. She ended up having fun showing off her new house in those pictures." To embellish the layout, she used cream paint to add a shabby chic look to the lovely papers and embellishments.

Dawn Taranto, Gilbert, Arizona

Supplies: Patterned papers (Chatterbox, Paper Adventures, Paper Loft, SEI); letter stickers, epoxy word sticker (Creative Imaginations); star tacks, flower (Chatterbox); metal photo corners (Carolee's Creations); key charm (Ink It!); decorative brads, oval label holder, foam letter stamps (Making Memories); brown and taupe cardstocks; staples; pink brads; brown stamping ink; lace trim; rickrack; mini buttons; white acrylic paint; pink ribbons

blueprint for our family home

Scrapbooking changes the way a photographer sees things. Sharon took these before she began scrapbooking, showing the house's progress but not including any family. "I only wish I could go back and take the photos all over again. We were all there, all the time. We reveled in each new stage." She used the spread to show and tell about the different stages of construction. A quote block including wood letters and strips, stamping, chalking and other elements captures Sharon's feelings perfectly.

Sharon Whitehead, Vernon,
British Columbia, Canada

Supplies: Wooden letters (Westrim); letter stamps (Stampendous!); black mesh (Magic Mesh); metal letters, jump rings (Making Memories); brads (Karen Foster Design); epoxy number stickers (K & Company); ribbon (Memories and More); cream, butterscotch and mauve cardstocks (Bazzill); square punch (EK Success); balsa wood; spring green snaps; chalk; foam adhesive; acrylic paint; brown stamping ink; distress ink

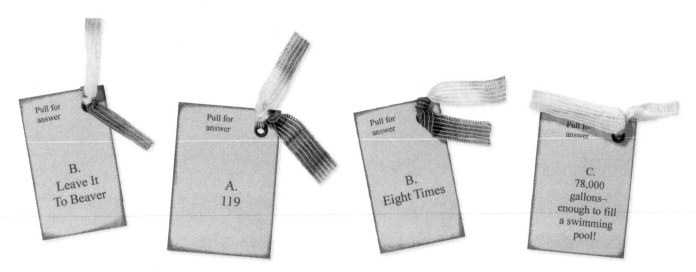

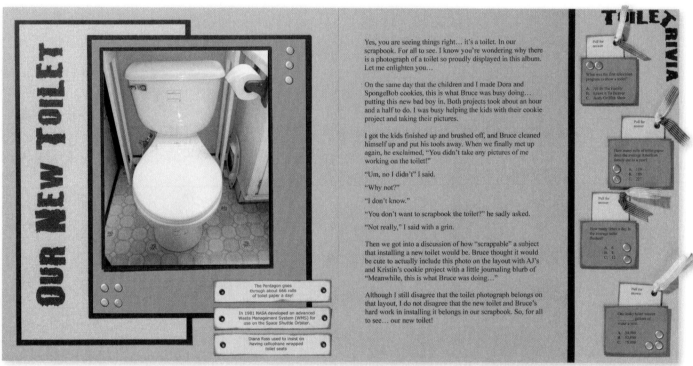

our new toilet

Ask and you shall receive. Not necessarily a toilet but a page about one. While Michelle took photos of her day making cookies with her children, her husband slaved away installing a new toilet. After he finished, he feigned being hurt that she only cropped the cookie making and not his project. As a joke, Michelle created this spread, complete with trivia and multiple-choice questions, found on the Internet. To design her page, Michelle placed her photo and journaling into a 12 x 12" computer document. When satisfied with the look, she created the hard copy, adding embellishments as needed.

Michelle Maret, South Bend, Indiana

Supplies: Putty, black, orange and sage cardstocks (Bazzill); ribbon (EK Success); gold flathead eyelets (Making Memories); green eyelets; brown stamping ink

in my room

Decorating a room shows part of our character during a certain stage in our life. Recently Cynthia found photos of her old room in her parents' house, and she created this page to showcase it. She says that when she saw the photos, "the memories of my haven came flooding back. I loved my room filled with my girly things!" Her page elements complemented the colors in her room photos with vibrant papers and stickers. The large silk flower adds a punch of the deepest pink and ties together all the page pieces.

Cynthia Baula Roybal, Las Vegas, Nevada

Supplies: Patterned paper, letter stickers (Doodlebug Design); polka-dot ribbon (Michaels); silk flower (Wal-Mart); large and medium circle punches (EK Success); concho letter (Jo-Ann Stores); white and black cardstocks; rickrack; small circle die cut

art

After Jenn and her husband showed an art gallery representative photos of their furniture and room colors, she recommended these art pieces to them. They brought them home to try them out with the decor and Jenn says, "I was in love, and I had to have them. They just spoke to me. I loved the mix of colors, the funky design and the boldness of the lines." After Jenn experimented with depth of field on a new camera, she created this page. She added simple graphic embellishments to finish the look.

Jenn Brookover, San Antonio, Texas

Supplies: Patterned papers (Daisy D's, Scenic Route Paper Co.); Rhonna Farrer's Sweet Pea Kit digital background (www.twopeasinabucket.com); wooden letters (Westrim); ribbons (Making Memories, May Arts); paper flower and decorative brad (Making Memories); acrylic letters (KI Memories); black and brown stamping inks

out of africa

After receiving a treasure box full of African artifacts from friends who had moved to Nigeria, Pamela and her husband were inspired to create a new look for their master bedroom. As they worked to change the room, other friends got into the act and added to their collection. She says, "Almost everything in the room was a gift from someone, making it a true family affair. Pamela's spread highlights the stunning African keepsakes and shares the stories behind the pieces.

Pamela James, Ventura, California

Supplies: Die-cut machine (Wishblade); taupe, cocoa, putty, orange and green cardstocks (Bazzill); brown stamping ink

behind closed doors

Diana created a mini album to showcase the most-lived-in rooms of her family's home. Among these is the refurbished basement where, she says, "We spend so much time down there sometimes I think if there were a kitchen we'd never come up." Diana included photos of her family eating dinner, playing games and snuggling close to each other on the coach—proving that true wealth is not in a family's possessions but in each other. Filmstrip frames, bottle cap letters and denim tags add a creative touch to her pages.

Diana Graham, Barrington, Illinois

Supplies: Patterned paper (Flair Designs, Rusty Pickle); ledger paper, safety pins, leather flower, rub-on letters (Making Memories); letter stickers (Chatterbox); natural tags/files (Autumn Leaves); bottle cap letters, chipboard frame, chipboard letters (Li'l Davis Designs); place tag (source unknown); ribbons (Making Memories, Must Be, Offray); woven labels (Creative Imaginations, Making Memories, Me & My Big Ideas); filmstrip frames (Creative Imaginations)

family pets

CHAPTER SEVEN

Furry, four-legged pals and other creatures of the animal kingdom have always had a special place in the family. Ever-devoted, always animated and never judgmental, they can make us laugh at their silly stunts while teaching us some of life's greatest lessons.

Our canine comrades are dynamic and full of life, whether they are greeting us at the door after work or jumping for a tennis ball that they will gleefully return again and again. Our feline friends may flaunt a more independent existence, but no one can argue that they are playful, lovable and will repeatedly meow for our affection. Free-flying birds, multi-colored aquarium fish, furry hamsters, gerbils and ferrets, proud and handsome horses and even snakes, lizards, spiders and scorpions will steal our hearts with their zany behavior and unique personalities.

Featuring beloved animal companions in scrapbooks does not take any fuzzy logic. It's easy to capture snapshots of animal life one woof or sniff at a time. So unleash your creativity and craft new-fangled pages that celebrate your pet.

One day my husband and daughter took our dog to the Laundry Mutt for a bath. They brought home a clean dog and another little surprise—a kitten from the pet rescue that we named Brother Bear.

—Sheila Doherty

"Animals
are such agreeable friends
- they ask no questions, they pass no criticisms."
—George Eliot

Problem: Rebekah wants a cat.

Solution: Dad promises her a cat at some later date, like after we move to our new home, hoping she'll forget or lose interest.

Problem: We've moved and Rebekah STILL wants a cat. Hasn't forgotten.

Solution: Put her off, saying we'll get one when our house is settled. Boxes still everywhere.

Problem: Mom REALLY doesn't want a cat knowing that regardless of promises to the contrary, she will be the one doing the cleaning up after said cat.

Solution: Rebekah promises to take care of the cat. Dad promises to cover for her.

Problem: We're settled into our new home and Rebekah STILL wants a cat.

Solution: Dad goes behind Mom's back and brings home a kitten.

SOLUTION

good

Problem: Mom is STILL not delighted with cat.

Solution: Rebekah feeds cat loyally every day. Dad takes c of clean up by buying a robotic litter box. Mom is happy. Rebekah is happy. Good solution.

my boys

Miriam and her husband have four daughters. So it's a good thing that their dog, Chaucer, is a boy. Miriam says, "Scott is completely devoted to his four daughters. He volunteers countless hours to youth sports, coaching our girls' . . . teams. But the dog is his 'boy' and he calls him that! I've rarely heard Scott call Chaucer by his real name. I've seen many . . . pages titled 'my boys,' and I just couldn't help myself!" Miriam's page features a color-blocked background with circles that she cut and inked with a makeup sponge.

Miriam Campbell, Olympia, Washington

Supplies: Pattered papers (Anna Griffin, Karen Foster Design, Paper Loft); metal letters (Jo-Ann Stores); circle punch, heart charm (EK Success); number charm (Li'l Davis Designs); label maker (Dymo); rub-on letters (Autumn Leaves); staples; pink brad; brown stamping ink

bernie and me

"In 2001, Bernie was a discarded puppy, dropped off on the road in front of our house. We took him in," Carolyn says, "and then he got terribly sick and we spent the winter and spring getting him healthy again. He's been my best friend since then." For being such a great companion and to celebrate her 54th birthday, Carolyn asked her husband to do a photo shoot of her with Bernie. To design her page, she used elements that a Web site put together as a kit.

Carolyn Cleveland, Maysville, Georgia

Supplies: Patterned papers, die cuts (KI Memories); letter stickers (C-Thru Ruler, KI Memories); phrase stickers (EK Success); brown and turquoise cardstocks; turquoise brads; brown stamping ink

signed, sealed, delivered

While searching online for the uncommon red piebald-colored miniature dachshund, Bonnie's family found a kennel in Montana. Through modern technology, they saw the puppies at two weeks, chose one at six weeks and waited for air transport at nine and a half weeks. Bonnie says, "You just don't know how excited we were to get our first peek at our new puppy . . . If you look closely, you can see that Emmie is getting her first peek at us, too. The photo . . . represented the exact instant we first glimpsed our future family member." Bonnie created her page using a monthly scrapbook kit with a postage theme.

Bonnie Perry, Vancouver, Washington

Supplies: Patterned papers, postage themed stamps (Club Scrap); foam letter stamps (Making Memories); metal-rimmed tag (Avery); red and khaki cardstocks; black brad; black and brown stamping inks; twill; pink and gray acrylic paints

all i need to know

Since Becky's son Adam "attends" an online academy for school, he doesn't get the typical school portraits, so Becky takes them. This year they decided to bring Winnie, their dog. "She needed a break and so did he, so they went off to play and explore," she says. "I just started taking some candid shots of the two of them, and this one was one of the results." A transparency she found communicated many of her feelings. She designed the page around it, picking up the colors in the photograph.

Becky Thompson, Fruitland, Idaho

Supplies: Printed transparency, stickers (Karen Foster Design); letter stamps (PSX Design); date stamp (Staples); red, green and khaki cardstocks; black stamping ink

my buddy

Bela created this page to celebrate the wonderful relationship she has with her dog, Bogey, and the years she waited for him. She grew up wanting a dog, and when she moved into her first apartment as a young adult, it was "pet-free." After she moved again, she and her husband chose Bogey from a litter of puppies. She says, "I picked you out of the bunch immediately. You seemed to have a spark about you." Bela designed this simple page with clean, crisp papers for a graphic look that focuses on the photo and journaling.

Bela Luis, Winnipeg, Manitoba, Canada
Photo: Joel Ross Photography, Winnipeg, Manitoba, Canada

Supplies: Quote sticker (Wordsworth); paw print charm (www.maudeandmillie.com); ribbons (May Arts, SEI); dog definitions paper (www.heatherannmeltzer.typepad.com); leather frames (Making Memories); metal word tag (Chronicle Books); brown, white and black cardstocks (Bazzill)

the way to know life

Beverly feels all kids should have a dog so, she says, "When my two daughters turned 3 and 8, I decided to get [a Westie]." She was familiar with the breed and felt it would be a good fit for her family. Queenie came when she was just 6 weeks old, and she and Autumn became immediate friends. Beverly's graphic design employs seemingly random letter stickers that spell out a quote she found. She anchors the page with ribbon that resembles a funky fashion belt.

Beverly Sizemore, Sulligent, Alabama

Supplies: Letter stickers, ribbon rings, ribbon (Li'l Davis Designs); die-cut letters (QuicKutz); red, white and black cardstocks; silver eyelets; black pen

julie

Sometimes when visiting the animal shelter, a puppy speaks to the heart. That's what happened to Nancy's family five years ago when they found Julie. "She was a puppy in a litter of eight. We fell in love with her because of her one floppy ear. She always looks like she is waiting for us to play." For this page, Nancy included various action shots of Julie doing the things she loves best, waiting to play and playing. She limited her colors to black and white with a spots of red and brown, allowing the photos to shine.

Nancy McCoy, Gulfport, Mississippi

Supplies: Foam letter stamps (Making Memories); paw buttons (Jesse James); red satin ribbon; buttons; black and white cardstocks; silver eyelets; white acrylic paint; red embroidery floss

two of a kind

Laura confesses that she was not much of a pet person until she met Thunder. On a trip to the Humane Society, she met a loud but adorable dog. She thought about him over the weekend, decided to adopt him and named him Thunder—because he was so loud. "I was lucky to find him that day. His personality is so quirky, and we're so much alike," she says. She enlarged the self-portrait photo and added the title on the bottom border.

Laura Stewart, Fort Wayne, Indiana

Supplies: Patterned paper (KI Memories); foam letter stamps, rub-on letters (Making Memories); letter stamps (PSX Design); green stamping ink; acrylic paint; green cardstock

things we could learn . . .

George has been a part of Maureen's family since he was a puppy. They adopted him from a rescue shelter six years ago. While Nate, her son, and George played in the back yard, "I followed [them] around for awhile and just kept shooting, which resulted in the great dog kiss picture," she says. Offering a few hints, she recommends taking many photos and she says, "Instead of saying 'say cheese,' say nothing and capture those unstaged moments." Her page features an enlarged photo of the sloppy dog kiss, surrounded by warm but neutral papers and embellishments.

Maureen Spell, Carlsbad, New Mexico

Supplies: Patterned papers (Daisy D's); mesh (Magic Mesh); printed transparency (Artistic Expressions); library card (Gaylord); label maker (Dymo); word button, woven label (Junkitz); photo turn (Making Memories); tan cardstock; orange brad; rust stamping ink; sandpaper; brown and white paint

best pals

Scrapbookers often use ingenuity to get the photos they want. After Sheila tried to get Casey, the family dog, to give doggy kisses to her son, Cody, she had a sudden inspiration. She says, "I went into the house and put a little bit of butter on my finger. I smeared it on Cody's cheek, turned the camera on, and the rest is history! Casey absolutely loved it, and Cody thought it was the funniest thing ever." To create her page, she designed a collage of patterned papers, distressed elements and various letter stickers.

Sheila Toppi, Lowell, Massachusetts

Supplies: Patterned papers (7 Gypsies, Carolee's Creations); acrylic letters (KI Memories); letter stickers (Sticker Studio); stencil letter, pog (Autumn Leaves); epoxy letter stickers (K & Company); negative strip transparency (Creative Imaginations); black brad; black stamping ink

buh!

Most scrapbookers have shared Bela's feelings of not having the best photo but still wanting to create the page. She says, "It is one of those that you're just happy to have in your scrapbook. The 'real' reason we scrapbook is for these memories to be captured." She enhanced a special moment in her son's little life with witty humor. The first word he spoke and clearly understood was not "mama" or "dada" as Bela hoped, but "Buh." Noah's name for Bogey, their dog. Her design uses warm browns, yellows and greens to give the page a cheerful, welcoming tone.

Bela Luis, Winnipeg, Manitoba, Canada

Supplies: Patterned paper (Chatterbox); letter stamps (FontWerks); metal-rimmed tag, definition sticker, mini safety pin (Making Memories); paw charm (www.maudeandmillie.com); ribbon (May Arts); mesh (Magic Mesh); brown, rust, mustard and white cardstocks; walnut ink; black and brown stamping inks

da boyz

"Barnabus was born right in my living room . . . I had to help Dixie deliver [him], and the moment I saw his little face I knew in my heart he was going to live with us forever," says Erika. "I just remember watching him grow for nine weeks and when it came time to sell his litter-mates, I just couldn't part with him." When designing pages, Erika likes to begin by randomly cutting papers. She then layers them on the page, adds her photos and fills in with journaling and embellishments.

Erika Hayes, Phoenix, Arizona

Supplies: Patterned papers, tags, red ribbon, die-cut tab (SEI); letter stickers (Sticker Studio); acrylic washer (Bazzill); rub-on letters (Doodlebug Design); ribbons (May Arts); brown stamping ink; rust and golden cardstocks; black pen

is that a dog at your table?

"I don't know when it started, but we all would be sitting at the dinner table, our conversations lingering well past the meal, and Schatzie, who would be under the table anyway, would find an open chair of someone who had left the table," says Jessie. "He would scoot out . . . and hop right on the chair, and sit there, just looking at us and almost nodding his head as if he were part of the conversation all along." Jessie used the colors of the era to create this humorous page.

Jessie Baldwin, Las Vegas, Nevada

Supplies: Patterned papers (Rusty Pickle); chipboard letters, frame (Li'l Davis Designs); ribbon; dark chocolate and white cardstocks

love that dog

Pets often become a true part of the family. That is certainly true in Kelli's house. Riley, a half golden retriever and half Labrador retriever was bred to be a guide dog. The breed professes sweet temperaments and a good "work ethic." Kelli says, "Riley was a rotten puppy, so he wasn't suitable as a guide dog, hence the name Riley from 'Life of Riley'—a life that is carefree and void of work." She created her layout using warm tones to coordinate with her photo and to emphasize the beautiful caramel color of Riley's fur.

Kelli Noto, Centennial, Colorado

Supplies: Patterned papers, tag (Basic Grey); letter die cuts (QuickKutz); twill letter tags (Carolee's Creations); caramel, cream and black cardstocks; ribbon; gray stamping ink

the power of a pet

"The kids begged to go over 'just to look'," says Valerie. The family was out on a Saturday morning, and they spotted a breeder showing off some puppies. "We all fell in love with the same sweet little girl, and I let my family talk me into getting her that day. We named her Sammi on the way home." Valerie combined photos taken at different times. For a more cohesive look she printed three in sepia tones and one in full color. Valerie dressed them up with blue and gold papers and embellishments.

Valerie Barton, Flowood, Mississippi

Supplies: Patterned papers (FontWerks); letter stamps (FontWerks, Hero Arts); letter tiles (Darice); photo turns (Making Memories); letter stickers (Mrs. Grossman's); black stamping ink; ribbon; turquoise brads; staples; transparency

reading with chicken

Birds definitely have their own personalities. Shortly after Leah and her husband brought Chicken home, they realized a couple of things about her. Leah says, "Whenever we brought her out of her cage, she'd eventually find newspapers or cookbooks lying around and just start munching. I think she likes the taste, sound and texture of crinkling paper, and destroying it makes her feel bigger." This page combines soft, colorful papers with descriptive photos and journaling.

Leah Blanco Williams, Rochester, New York

Supplies: Patterned papers (Fancy Pants Designs, Hot Off The Press); letter stickers (Basic Grey); photo corner stickers (Fancy Pants Designs); circle and square punches (Creative Memories); paper flowers (Prima); watercolor cocoa stamping ink (Tsukineko); date stamp (Making Memories); brown cardstock

enough already

Once upon a time, Trudy's family owned a dog and a cat. One day she and her children set sail on a ferry boat to visit a friend who had seven guinea pigs, one with babies. She says, "My kids fell in love with her guinea pigs, especially the babies, one of which was still looking for a home." She took this photo during their stay, and three weeks later, when the babies could leave their mother, Snowball was delivered to their home. Trudy used feminine colors and soft embellishments to honor both girls in the photo.

Trudy Sigurdson, Victoria, British Columbia, Canada

Supplies: Patterned paper (Sandylion); rickrack (Doodlebug Design); pink cheesecloth (Wimpole Street); rub-on letters (Chatterbox); acrylic heart (Heidi Swapp); bead word (Li'l Davis Designs); pink and white cardstocks; buttons

matt and gizmo

Lisa's husband went to purchase a gardening hat and came home with a kitten. He told the family she was a bonus to anyone buying a hat. Actually, he saw a sign over a small box that said "Free to a good home," and melted when he saw her adorable face. So he brought her home. "Of course, the kids fell in love with her as soon as they saw her. She had this funny way of moving her ears, and it reminded them of the Gremlins movie," she says, so they named her Gizmo. Lisa kept her layout masculine to highlight her son.

Lisa Turley, Chesapeake, Virginia

Supplies: Patterned papers (Blue Cardigan Designs); ribbons (Offray); buckle (Nunn Design); mosaic tiles and tags (Sarah Heidt Photo Craft); safety pin (Making Memories); mini gold brads (Creative Impressions); white and black cardstocks; white embroidery floss; spiral clip; black stamping ink; sandpaper; black pen

pick pocket?

As Tigger snoozed, Carolyn's husband pointed out how she had her paw in his pocket. Carolyn grabbed her camera and when the photo came back, the scrapbook page started forming in her mind. She says, "The first thing I thought of was that she was trying to pick his pocket, hoping there would be something for kitties in it. Then I imagined what she was hoping would be in the pocket—money, toys, a fish?" The page design flowed from there with images of money and a fish.

Carolyn Cleveland, Maysville, Georgia

Supplies: Patterned papers (Karen Foster Design, ScrapTherapy Designs); metal letter tags (Hirschberg, Schutz & Co.); stickers (Deluxe Designs, Imagination Project, Provo Craft, Sweetwater); decorative brad (Making Memories); printed twill sticker (All My Memories); blue twill, library pocket (Rather B' Scrappin); Asian coin (Club Scrap); twine; fabric; mini brads; black and brown stamping inks; spiral clip

2 friends

As Jennifer's daughter plunged into a hard-core, toddler snooze, a little furry friend joined her. "When I went into my daughter's room before bed to turn out her lamp, I saw this! It wasn't too long after we brought home the kitten." Jennifer took this photo without the flash to allow the light to remain soft. She chose soft, muted tones in her papers, stickers and acrylic paint to complement the photo.

Jennifer Johner, Asquith,
Saskatchewan, Canada

Supplies: Patterned papers, letter stickers (Basic Grey); foam letter stamps (Making Memories); flower clip (Scrapworks); fibers; cream cardstock; acrylic paint

my name is . . .

Naming a pet can be a calculated adventure or, in some cases, it can flow from the pet as he or she exhibits a personality. The latter is what happened when Kristin got to know her new kitten. Beginning as Tiny Tim, Kristin felt the cat needed a different name since he was sick. "I fell in love with the name Gryphon and I gave you the middle name Owynn because it means little fighter," she recounts in her journaling. It eventually morphed into Gryphon Nermyl or on special occasions, "Precious Gryphon Nermylstein."

Kristin Hill, Orlando, Florida

Supplies: Patterned paper (Chatterbox); label maker (Dymo); foam letter stamps, rub-on letters (Making Memories); slate and tan cardstocks (Bazzill); acrylic paint

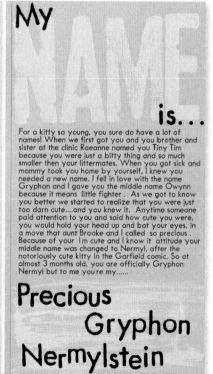

My **NAME** is...

For a kitty so young, you sure do have a lot of names! When we first got you and you brother and sister at the clinic Raeanne named you Tiny Tim because you were just a bitty thing and so much smaller then your littermates. When you got sick and mommy took you home by yourself, I knew you needed a new name. I fell in love with the name Gryphon and I gave you the middle name Owynn because it means little fighter . As we got to know you better we started to realize that you were just too darn cute....and you knew it. Anytime someone paid attention to you and said how cute you were, you would hold your head up and bat your eyes. in a move that aunt Brooke and I called so precious . Because of your Im cute and I know it attitude your middle name was changed to Nermyl. after the notoriously cute kitty in the Garfield comic. So at almost 3 months old, you are officially Gryphon Nermyl but to me you're my......

Precious Gryphon Nermylstein

perfect peaches

Friends of Donna's family found a stray cat; they wanted to keep her but a family member was allergic. They gave the kitten to Donna's family who had in previous months lost another cat. Life with this new member of the family was not without some tension. Donna's kids feared the cat "when she goes into 'play' mode," she says. At the same time they make sure their mom knows they don't want to give her back. Donna took photos of Peaches sleeping by the window and used earthy colors with accents in black to design her page.

Donna Manning, Huntsville, Texas

Supplies: Patterned papers (DMD); letter stickers (Creative Imaginations); label maker (Dymo); black and avocado cardstocks (Bazzill); square punches

a bump in the bed

Colleen thought she had made the bed but noticed the sheet bunched up. When she gave the sheet a tug, she heard a stark meow from her cat who had been sleeping under the covers. For her design, Colleen says, "I wanted to keep the page whimsical and fun, just like the memory I was recording." She accomplished this by mimicking the bed bump by creating a curved title using image-editing software.

Colleen O'Toole, Tucson, Arizona

Supplies: Patterned paper (American Crafts); buttons (SEI); corner rounder, circle cutting system (Creative Memories); image-editing software (Jasc Paintshop Pro); cream and red cardstocks

girlfriends

As a pet ages, one must face that she won't live forever. Tammy created this layout to "reflect upon the friendship I've had with my furry friend of 17 years." Her journaling tells a bit of the life story of her cat, beginning with finding her father "in some pricker bushes down at Sandy Beach." The story continues with her being born in Tammy's home and living with her ever since. She chose vibrant citrus colors to accent the cat's fur and the leaves surrounding her.

Tammy Mellish, Bellow Falls, Vermont

Supplies: Patterned paper (Chatterbox, KI Memories); ribbons (May Arts, Offray); library pocket (Boxer Scrapbook Productions); postage stamp sticker (Scrapping With Style); metal word, flowers, definition (Making Memories); woven label (Me & My Big Ideas); white, orange and tan cardstocks; orange flathead eyelets; yellow acrylic paint; green stamping ink

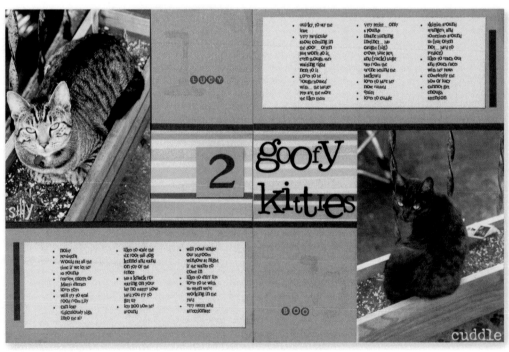

2 goofy kitties

Julia has a handle on her two cats' personalities, and she created this layout to demonstrate it. Each page features a cat sitting in a planter box. Designing primarily with orange, Julia created two similar sides of the layout. She put the photos and text boxes in opposite corners and added a striped box to carry the title over the page split. Each box holds a list of contrasting traits. Lucy "has a knack for staying on your lap no matter how hard you try to get up," Julia says. Boo "loves to have her nose rubbed."

Julia Richert, Astoria, Oregon

Supplies: Patterned vellum (American Crafts); letter stamps (Making Memories, Ma Vinci's Reliquary, PSX Design); letter stickers (Doodlebug Design); word stickers (Bo-Bunny Press); black, orange and pumpkin cardstocks; stamping inks

playmates

Kathy created a mini album about the family beagle, Belle. Each spread features how Belle relates to a child in the family. Kathy says, "It is really funny because she seems to know what each child's personality is and her behavior with that child matches accordingly. My son Hayden is rough and tumble and she will play with him . . . Morgan is older and she sleeps with her at night . . . Isaac is the youngest and likes to cuddle with Belle." Each mini spread takes on the personality of the relationship the pair shares.

Kathy Fesmire, Athens, Tennessee

Supplies: Patterned papers (Daisy D's, Imagination Project, Memories Complete, Miss Elizabeth's, Scenic Route Paper Co., Suzy's Zoo, Westrim); foam letter stamps (Duncan); dog die cuts (Leaving Prints); rub-on letters, rub-on words (DieCuts with a View, Making Memories, Westrim); heart tile (Hirschberg, Schutz & Co.); letter beads (Beadery); date stamp (Leisure Arts); ribbon (Offray); paint chip, paper scuffer (PM Designs); number stamps (Plaid); flowers, decorative brads (Making Memories); globe, ruler and pencil charms (Crafts, Etc.); die-cut letters (Ellison); olive and white cardstocks; buttons; small dog bone charms; black and red stamping inks; green and black acrylic paints

additional credits and sources

Cover

Lasting Memories

Jumping on the bed is a regular family activity in this household! The photographs express family love and laughter in this joyful family layout. Jodi used cranberry, cream and a few shades of blue to perfectly complement the colors in the photos. She handcut the title onto cranberry and navy blue cardstocks and created her own flower embellishments by combining silk flowers with fabric-covered buttons.

Jodi Amidei, Memory Makers Books
Photos: Kelli Noto, Centennial, Colorado

Supplies: Patterned papers (C-Thru Ruler, Making Memories, NRN Designs); ribbon (Offray); buttons (Prym-Dritz); eyelets (Family Treasures); watermark ink (Tsukineko); silk flowers (Bloomin' Blossoms); cardstock; fabric; vellum; chalk ink; stamping ink

Page 3
Bookplate

This bookplate speaks country-charm in every way. Inked patterned papers in cranberry, cream and blue harmonize with the dainty silk flower embellishments and sheer ribbon.

Jodi Amidei, Memory Makers Books

Supplies: Patterned papers (C-Thru Ruler, Making Memories, NRN Designs); silk flowers (Bloomin' Blossoms); buttons (Prym-Dritz); watermark ink (Tsukineko); fabric; chalk ink; stamping ink

Page 7
Home Is Where Your Story Begins

Lydia created a page about the first place she lived with her husband—a Victorian home built in 1894. Her journaling includes details about the house and the surrounding neighborhood that she loved. Her title was created with a design program by creating separate text boxes for the large and smaller words. She adjusted the color of the word "home" and layered the two boxes on top of one another. Premade key and keyhole embellishments fit the era in which the home was built.

Lydia Rueger, Memory Makers Books

Supplies: Patterned paper (Anna Griffin); key and keyhole embellishments (Li'l Davis Designs); image-editing software (Adobe InDesign); transparency; acrylic paint

Page 8
Hammond Family

A family dinner provided the perfect photo op for the Hammond family. Torrey used a combination of patterned papers, cardstock stickers and printed twill to express the theme of family. A metal tag woven through the twill and the capital "H" add dimension to the layout.

Torrey Scott, Thornton, Colorado
Photo: Bruce Aldridge, Broomfield, Colorado

Supplies: Patterned papers, stickers, metal tag (Flair Designs); printed twill (Creative Impressions); letter and number stamps (PSX Design); distress ink (Ranger); brads (Provo Craft); chalk ink

Page 9

Albums: Pioneer, Westrim. Paper: Crossed Paths, Masterpiece Studios. Embellishments: All My Memories, Crossed Paths, Hot Off The Press, KI Memories. Adhesives: EK Success, Glue Dots International, Tombow. Pens and markers: EK Success, Marvy, Staedtler

Page 10

Quotes, Phrases & Sayings: American Traditional Designs, Flair Designs

Page 11
You're Invited

Torrey created an invitation and name tag perfect for any family gathering, whether it be a small five-person dinner or a mammoth family reunion. She adhered small blocks of family-themed patterned paper onto a multicolored background and added blue brads to accent.

Torrey Scott, Thornton, Colorado

Supplies: Mosaic card (DMD); patterned paper (Flair Designs); mini brads; rust marker; black pen

Page 13
Proud

Jeniece created a layout to honor her mother-in-law who accomplished her goal of graduating from college. Chalkboard tags work well to spell the title and also to convey the theme of education. Fabric, twill, ribbons and a piece of the commencement program add dimension and serve as the perfect accents to the layout.

Jeniece Higgins, Lake Forest, Illinois

Supplies: Patterned paper (C-Thru Ruler, Rusty Pickle); letter stamps (PSX Design, Stampin' Up!); stickers (Making Memories); tab (Melissa Frances); chalkboard tags (Pottery Barn); ribbon; fabric; library pocket; staples; stamping ink

Page 29
Dad

Danielle pays special tribute to her dad in this layout. She used a photo taken of her as a toddler at a trip to Sea World as the focal point and added smaller pictures of her and her dad from present day. She says, "I love comparing the photos from the two different time periods in both of our lives. I love thinking about how far we've come together and what a big part he's played in my life." Her journaling is a unique combination of her own handwriting and letter stamps. Green, blue and brown buttons and a brass picture hanger add artistic flair to her layout.

Danielle Thompson, Tucker, Georgia

Supplies: Patterned papers (Basic Grey, EK Success, KI Memories, Kopp Design, Scrapworks, 7 Gypsies); buttons (Junkitz, Wal-Mart, Le Bouton); brass picture hanger (Home Depot); stamps (Scrappy Cat, Ma Vinci's Reliquary); embroidery floss (DMC); chipboard letters (Li'l Davis Designs); chalk (Craf-T); stamping ink

Page 45
Family Quilt

Denise's layout symbolizes how each member of her family is like a piece of a traditional homemade quilt. Her journaling shares how she and her husband were happy loving their dog, Heidi, and didn't foresee children on the horizon. Fifteen years and four children later, she says, "To think we couldn't love anyone more than we loved our dog is just laughable at this point in our lives. Our family is now complete." She printed her journaling onto fabric and added lace, ribbon and vintage buttons to give her layout a warm feeling.

Denise Tucker, Versailles, Indiana
Photos: Huddle Photography, Galesburg, Illinois; Jerry Hunter Photography, Madison, Indiana; Olan Mills Photo Studio, Greensburg, Indiana; Lifetouch, Galion, Ohio

Supplies: Chipboard frame (Rusty Pickle); decorative metal corners (Eggery Place); rivets (Chatterbox); ribbon (Offray); silver leafing pen (Krylon); number stickers (Foofala); distress ink (Ranger); acrylic paint; fabric; lace; vintage buttons

Page 61
Coat Hangers & Colouring Books

Trudy created a layout to celebrate her beloved Great Aunty Olwen. She wanted to convey this British lady's colorful and quirky personality that was most often seen in her gifts. She says, "My most vivid childhood memories of Aunty Olwen was when she gave my brother and me coat hangers as a gift. This was so typical of her, and I wanted to make a layout that showed her colorful personality." Rickrack, silk flowers, page pebbles, ribbons and buttons perfectly complement the pink and green patterned papers.

Trudy Sigurdson, Victoria, British Columbia
Photos: Phyllis Wright, Victoria,
British Columbia, Canada

Supplies: Patterned papers, tags, letter stickers (Basic Grey); rickrack (Paper Daisy); green ribbon (Offray); pink ribbon, photo turns (Making Memories); silk flowers (Michaels); buttons (Jesse James); mini page pebbles, letter stamps (Memories in the Making); brads; transparency

Page 77

A Reunion Like No Other

Jessie created a page using a photo of her entire family taken on the island of Vieques in Puerto Rico, her grandfather's homeland. She says, "It is amazing that 80 years later, the infant great-grand-son of Luis Hernandez could rock to sleep on the same beach, under the same stars, listening to the same waves. And equally amazing that we could get a family photo of all of us smiling and looking in the same direction!" Crimped handmade paper and small metallic seashell accents complement the oceanside photo.

Jessie Baldwin, Las Vegas, Nevada
Photo: Jared Seger Photography,
Portland, Oregon

Supplies: Patterned papers (Me & My Big Ideas); handmade paper (Janlynn); metal accents (Nunn Design); transparency

Page 97

Our Home

Samantha's page is a photo montage of the remodeling changes she and her husband made to their home. She says, "I took the photos at night to create a warm, homey feeling. The incandescent lights create a soft, yellow glow." Samantha chose to keep her embellishments simple to not overcrowd the selection of photos. Paragraph-style journaling tells the story of her home's remodeling project.

Samantha Walker, Battle Ground, Washington

Supplies: Image-editing software (Adobe); tag die/emboss plate (Spellbinders Paper Arts); decorative brads, date stamp, silk flowers, leather bookplate (Making Memories); cardstocks; chiffon ribbon; red eyelet; black stamping ink; embroidery thread

Page 109

Good Solution

Sheila's layout features a large focal-point photo of her daughter with her new kitten, Brother Bear. She employed a clever technique in her journaling by posing "Problem" and "Solution" statements to convey her initial reluctance and eventual satisfaction with the family kitten. She chose patterned papers that bring out the rich vibrance of her daughter's shirt in the photo.

Sheila Doherty, Coeur d'Alene, Idaho

Supplies: Patterned papers (Carolee's Creations, Creative Imaginations, KI Memories); foam letter stamps (Making Memories); chipboard letter (Li'l Davis Designs); rub-on letters (Scrapworks); ribbon (Michaels); acyric paint

sOurCe guide

The following companies manufacture products featured in this book. Please check your local retailers to find these materials, or go to a company's Web site for the latest product. In addition, we have made every attempt to properly credit the items mentioned in this book. We apologize to any company that we have listed incorrectly, and we would appreciate hearing from you.

2DYE4
www.canscrapink.com

3M
(800) 364-3577
www.3m.com

7 Gypsies
(800) 588-6707
www.7gypsies.com

A.C. Moore
www.acmoore.com

Accu-Cut®
(800) 288-1670
www.accucut.com

Adobe Systems Incorporated
(866) 766-2256
www.adobe.com

All My Memories
(888) 553-1998
www.allmymemories.com

All Night Media - (see Plaid Enterprises)

Altered Pages
(405) 360-1185
www.alteredpages.com

American Crafts
(800) 879-5185
www.americancrafts.com

American Stamps - no contact info

American Tag Company
(800) 223-3956
www.americantag.net

American Traditional Designs®
(800) 448-6656
www.americantraditional.com

Anchor - no contact info

Anna Griffin, Inc.
(888) 817-8170
www.annagriffin.com

AOL (America Online)
www.aol.com

Arctic Frog
(479) 636-FROG
www.arcticfrog.com

Artistic Expressions
(219) 764-5158
www.artisticexpressionsinc.com

Autumn Leaves
(800) 588-6707
www.autumnleaves.com

Avery Dennison Corporation
(800) GO-AVERY
www.avery.com

Basic Grey™
(801) 451-6006
www.basicgrey.com

Bazzill Basics Paper
(480) 558-8557
www.bazzillbasics.com

Beadery®, The
(401) 539-2432
www.thebeadery.com

Blooming' Blossoms - no contact info

Blue Cardigan Designs
(770) 904-4320
www.bluecardigan.com

Bo-Bunny Press
(801) 771-4010
www.bobunny.com

Bobbin Robin - no contact info

Boutique Trims, Inc.
(248) 437-2017
www.boutiquetrims.com

Boxer Scrapbook Productions
(503) 625-0455
www.boxerscrapbooks.com

Canson®, Inc.
(800) 628-9283
www.canson-us.com

Card Connection - see Michaels

Carolee's Creations®
(435) 563-1100
www.ccpaper.com

ChartPak
(800) 628-1910
www.chartpak.com

Chatterbox, Inc.
(208) 939-9133
www.chatterboxinc.com

Chronicle Books
(800) 722-6656
www.chroniclebooks.com

Clearsnap, Inc.
(800) 448-4862
www.clearsnap.com

Clorox Company, The
www.thecloroxcompany.com

Close To My Heart®
(888) 655-6552
www.closetomyheart.com

Cloud 9 Design
(763) 493-0990
www.cloud9design.biz

Club Scrap™, Inc.
(888) 634-9100
www.clubscrap.com

Colorbök™, Inc.
(800) 366-4660
www.colorbok.com

Comotion Rubber Stamps- see Uptown Design Company

CottageArts.net™
www.cottagearts.net

Craf-T Products
(507) 235-3996
www.craf-tproducts.com

Crafts, Etc.
(800) 888-0321
www.craftsetc.com

Creative Imaginations
(800) 942-6487
www.cigift.com

Creative Impressions Rubber Stamps
(719) 596-4860
www.creativeimpressions.com

Creative Memories®
(800) 468-9335
www.creativememories.com

Crossed Paths™
(972) 393-3755
www.crossedpaths.net

Daisy D's Paper Company
(888) 601-8955
www.daisydspaper.com

Darice, Inc.
(800) 321-1494
www.darice.com

Delta Technical Coatings, Inc.
(800) 423-4135
www.deltacrafts.com

Deluxe Designs
(480) 497-9005
www.deluxedesigns.com

Designer's Library by Lana, The
(660) 582-6484
www.thedesignerslibrary.com

Diane's Daughters®
(801) 621-8392
www.dianesdaughters.com

DieCuts with a View™
(877) 221-6107
www.dcwv.com

DMC Corp.
(973) 589-0606
www.dmc.com

DMD Industries, Inc.
(800) 805-9890
www.dmdind.com

Doodlebug Design™ Inc.
(801) 966-9952
www.doodlebugdesigninc.com

Dover Publications, Inc.
(800) 223-3130
www.doverpublications.com

Duncan Enterprises
(800) 782-6748
www.duncan-enterprises.com

Dymo
www.dymo.com

Eggery Place, The
www.theeggeryplace.com

EK Success™, Ltd.
(800) 524-1349
www.eksuccess.com

Ellison® Craft & Design
(800) 253-2238
www.ellison.com

Emagination Crafts, inc.
(866) 238-9770
www.emaginationcrafts.com

Eyelet Outlet - no contact info

Family Treasures, Inc.®
www.familytreasures.com

Fancy Pants Designs, LLC
(801) 779-3212
www.fancypantsdesigns.com

FiberMark
(802) 257-0365
http://scrapbook.fibermark.com

Fibers by the Yard™
(405) 364-8066
www.fibersbytheyard.com

Fiskars®, Inc.
(800) 950-0203
www.fiskars.com

Flair® Designs
(888) 546-9990
www.flairdesignsinc.com

FontWerks
www.fontwerks.com

FoofaLa
(402) 330-3208
www.foofala.com

Frances Meyer, Inc.®
(413) 584-5446
www.francesmeyer.com

Gaylord Bros.
(800) 634-6307
www.gaylord.com

Glue Dots® International
(888) 688-7131
www.gluedots.com

Go West Studios
(214) 227-0007
www.goweststudios.com

Grafix®
(800) 447-2349
www.grafix.com

Graphic Products Corporation
(800) 323-1660
www.gpcpapers.com

Great Balls of Fiber
(303) 697-5942
www.greatballsoffiber.com

Halcraft USA
(212) 376-1580
www.halcraft.com

Happy Hammer, The
(303) 690-3883
www.thehappyhammer.com

Heidi Grace Designs
(866) 89heidi
www.heidigrace.com

Heidi Swapp/Advantus Corporation
(904) 482-0092
www.heidiswapp.com

Hero Arts® Rubber Stamps, Inc.
(800) 822-4376
www.heroarts.com

Hillcreek Designs
(619) 562-5799
www.hillcreekdesigns.com

Hirschberg Schutz & Co., Inc.
(800) 221-8640

Hobby Lobby Stores, Inc.
www.hobbylobby.com

Home Depot
www.homedepot.com

Homemade Memories - no contact info

Hot Off The Press, Inc.
(800) 227-9595
www.paperpizazz.com

Houston Art, Inc. - no contact info

Imagination Project, Inc.
(513) 860-2711
www.imaginationproject.com

Impress Rubber Stamps
(206) 901-9101
www.impressrubberstamps.com

Ink It! - no contact info

Inkadinkado® Rubber Stamps
(800) 888-4652
www.inkadinkado.com

Janlynn® Corporation of America
(800) 445-5565
www.janlynn.com

Jasc Software
(800) 622-2793
www.jasc.com

Jennifer Collection, The
(518) 272-4572
www.paperdiva.net

Jesse James & Co., Inc.
(610) 435-0201
www.jessejamesbutton.com

Jest Charming
(702) 564-5101
www.jestcharming.com

Jo-Ann Stores
(888) 739-4120
www.joann.com

June Taylor - no contact info

Junkitz™
(732) 792-1108
www.junkitz.com

K & Company
(888) 244-2083
www.kandcompany.com

Karen Foster Design
(801) 451-9779
www.karenfosterdesign.com

KI Memories
(972) 243-5595
www.kimemories.com

Kopp Design
(801) 489-6011
www.koppdesign.com

Krylon®
(216) 566-2000
www.krylon.com

La Petites - no contact info

Lay Over - no contact info

LazerLetterz
(281) 627-4227
www.lazerletterz.com

Leaving Prints™
(801) 426-0636
www.leavingprints.com

Le Bouton - no contact info

Li'l Davis Designs
(949) 838-0344
www.lildavisdesigns.com

Lion Brand Yarn Company
www.lionbrand.com

Little Black Dress Designs
(360) 894-8844
www.littleblackdressdesigns.com

Lost Coast Designs
(408) 244-2777
www.lost-coast-designs.com

Ma Vinci's Reliquary
http://crafts.dm.net/mall/reliquary/

Magenta Rubber Stamps
(800) 565-5254
www.magentastyle.com

Magic Mesh
(651) 345-6374
www.magicmesh.com

Magic Scraps™
(972) 385-1838
www.magicscraps.com

Making Memories
(800) 286-5263
www.makingmemories.com

Marcel Schurman
(800) 333-6724
www.schurmanfinepapers.com

Marvy® Uchida/ Uchida of America, Corp.
(800) 541-5877
www.uchida.com

Masterpiece Studios
(800) 447-0219
www.masterpiecestudios.com

May Arts
(800) 442-3950
www.mayarts.com

me & my BiG ideas®
(949) 883-2065
www.meandmybigideas.com

Melissa Frances/Heart & Home, Inc.
(905) 686-9031
www.melissafrances.com

Memories Complete™, LLC
(866) 966-6365
www.memoriescomplete.com

Memories in the Making/Leisure Arts
(800) 643-8030
www.leisurearts.com

Michaels® Arts & Crafts
(800) 642-4235
www.michaels.com

Microsoft Corporation
www.microsoft.com

Midori
(800) 659-3049
www.midoriribbon.com

Miss Elizabeth's™
www.dollartree.com

Mrs. Grossman's Paper Company
(800) 429-4549
www.mrsgrossmans.com

Mustard Moon™
(408) 299-8542
www.mustardmoon.com

My Mind's Eye™, Inc.
(800) 665-5116
www.frame-ups.com

Nicole, Inc. - no contact info

NRN Designs
(800) 421-6958
www.nrndesigns.com

Nunn Design
(360) 379-3557
www.nunndesign.com

Office Depot
www.officedepot.com

Office Max
www.officemax.com

Offray
www.offray.com

On The Surface
(847) 675-2520

Out There Scrapbooking - no contact info

Outdoors & More Scrapbook Decor
(801) 390-6919
www.outdoorsandmore.com

Paper Adventures®
(800) 525-3196
www.paperadventures.com

Paper Co., The/ANW Crestwood
(800) 525-3196
www.anwcrestwood.com

Paper Connection, The - no contact info

Paper Daisy, The - no contact info

Paper Fever, Inc.
(800) 477-0902
www.paperfever.com

Paper Inspirations™
(406) 756-9678
www.paperinspirations.com

Paper Loft
(866) 254-1961
www.paperloft.com

Pebbles Inc.
(801) 224-1857
www.pebblesinc.com

Pepperell Braiding Company
(800) 343-8114
www.pepperell.com

Pioneer Photo Albums, Inc.®
(800) 366-3686
www.pioneerphotoalbums.com

Plaid Enterprises, Inc.
(800) 842-4197
www.plaidonline.com

PM designs
(888) 595-2887
www.designsbypm.com

Postmodern Design
(405) 321-3176
www.stampdiva.com

Pottery Barn
www.potterybarn.com

Prickley Pear Rubber Stamps
www.prickleypear.com

Prima
(909) 627-5532
www.mulberrypaperflowers.com

Provo Craft®
(888) 577-3545
www.provocraft.com

Prym-Dritz Corporation
www.dritz.com

PSX Design™
(800) 782-6748
www.psxdesign.com

Pulsar Paper Products
(877) 861-0031

Punch Bunch, The
(254) 791-4209
www.thepunchbunch.com

Purple Onion Designs
www.purpleoniondesigns.com

QuicKutz
(801) 765-1144
www.quickutz.com

Ranger Industries, Inc.
(800) 244-2211
www.rangerink.com

Rather B' Scrappin
(708) 496-8795
www.ratherbscrappin.com

Remember When - no contact info

Royal Talens
www.talens.com

Rusty Pickle
(801) 746-1045
www.rustypickle.com

Sakura Hobby Craft
(310) 212-7878
www.sakuracraft.com

Sandylion Sticker Designs
(800) 387-4215
www.sandylion.com

Sarah Heidt Photo Craft, LLC
(734) 424-2776
www.sarahheidtphotocraft.com

Sassafras Lass
(801) 269-1331
www.sassafraslass.com

Savage Universal Corporation
(800) 624-8891
www.savagepaper.com

Scenic Route Paper Co.
(801) 785-0761
www.scenicroutepaper.com

Scrapbook Sensation - no contact info

Scrapbook Wizard™, The
(435) 752-7555
www.scrapbookwizard.com

Scrapping With Style
(704) 254-6238
www.scrappingwithstyle.com

Scrappy Cat™, LLC
(440) 234-4850
www.scrappycatcreations.com

ScrapTherapy Designs, Inc.
(800) 333-7880
www.scraptherapy.com

Scrapworks, LLC
(801) 363-1010
www.scrapworks.com

SEI, Inc.
(800) 333-3279
www.shopsei.com

Sizzix®
(866) 742-4447
www.sizzix.com

Spellbinders™ Paper Arts, LLC
(888) 547-0400
www.spellbinders.us

Staedtler®, Inc.
(800) 927-7723
www.staedtler.us

Stamp Craft - see Plaid Enterprises

Stampabilities®
(800) 888-0321
www.stampabilities.com

Stampendous!®
(800) 869-0474
www.stampendous.com

Stampin' Up!®
(800) 782-6787
www.stampinup.com

Staples, Inc.
(800) 3STAPLE
www.staples.com

Sticker Studio™
(208) 322-2465
www.stickerstudio.com

Sunday International
(800) 401-8644
www.sundayint.com

Suzy's Zoo®
(800) 777-4846
www.suzyszoo.com

Sweetwater
(800) 359-3094
www.sweetwaterscrapbook.com

Target
www.target.com

Timeless Touches™/Dove Valley Productions, LLC
(623) 362-8285
www.timelesstouches.net

Tombow®
(800) 835-3232
www.tombowusa.com

Treehouse Designs
(501) 372-1109
www.treehouse-designs.com

Tsukineko®, Inc.
(800) 769-6633
www.tsukineko.com

Turtle Press
(206) 706-3186
www.turtlearts.com

Uptown Design Company™, The
(800) 888-3212
www.uptowndesign.com

USArtQuest, Inc.
(517) 522-6225
www.usartquest.com

Wallies
(802)492-3436
www.wallies.com

Wal-Mart Stores, Inc.
(800) WALMART
www.walmart.com

Westrim® Crafts
(800) 727-2727
www.westrimcrafts.com

Wimpole St. - no contact info

Wishblade™, Inc.
(651) 644-5144
www.wishblade.com

Wordsworth
(719) 282-3495
www.wordsworthstamps.com

Wübie Prints
(888) 256-0107
www.wubieprints.com

Wrights® Ribbon Accents
(877) 597-4448
www.wrights.com

Xpressions - no contact info

index